YOU CAN TOO!

A Mind, Body, Spirit Connection for Weight Loss

You Can Too!

A Mind, Body, Spirit Connection for Weight Loss

Jacqueline Garrick
ACSW, CSW, BCETS, CPT

Illustrated by
Fred Harper

RP
Resilient Press

You Can Too!
by Jacqueline Garrick

Important Note: Every effort has been made to ensure that the information contained in this book is complete and accurate. However, neither the publisher nor the author is engaged in rendering professional advice or services to individuals. The ideas, techniques, tips, procedures, and suggestions contained in this book are not intended as a substitute for seeking medical attention. All matters regarding your health require professional medical supervision. Neither the author nor the publisher shall be liable or responsible for any loss or damage allegedly arising from any information or suggestion in this book. The opinions expressed in this book represent personal views of the author and not of the publisher. While the author has made every effort to provide accurate telephone and Internet references at the time of publication, neither the publisher nor the author assumes any responsibility for errors, or for changes that occur after publication.

Library of Congress Control Number: 2005904006
ISBN: 0-9714020-9-4

Published by Resilient Press
11921 Georgia Avenue
PO Box 130
Wheaton, MD 20902
FAX: 301-570-2279
Online: *www.YC2.org*

Cover and text design and production by Mulberry Tree Press, Inc.

Printed and bound in the United States of America

Contents

To my mom,

who has made 29 look great at every age

Acknowledgments

I WOULD NOT HAVE WRITTEN this book if it weren't for all of the people who seemed so interested and curious about what I did to lose weight. The questions I encountered about my eating habits, exercise, health, and genetics made me really stop and think about what was working for me, and what I tried and hated. When I was the Deputy Director for Health Care at the American Legion, my experiences in health policy, most specifically in performance measurement and lessons learned, taught me to keep a log of what worked and what were important contributing factors to my success. While at the Legion, Robert Hite, a health policy analyst, challenged my program evaluation and performance measurement skills, which I had not used much since graduate school. He became a touchstone for many of my life's decisions, and I am grateful to him in so many ways. The need to log and track my activities to see what was helping me lose weight was surely inspired by our many conversations about healthcare value. But, it was author and publisher Charlene Edwards who first encouraged me to write this book. She became my publishing consultant and advised me every step of the way and never let me quit. I am also very grateful to renowned trauma expert Dr. Mary Beth Williams, who first read a draft of my manuscript and provided an initial round of peer review and editing, not to mention her years of friendship and willingness to have adventures. Once she liked the manuscript, I felt encouraged to continue the process.

Joe Gannon, who did the layout for the book design and production, was an enormous help. He gave me a great deal of advice and guidance on how to publish. He and the rest of Mulberry Tree Press did an amazing job in creating this book.

When I needed a copy editor, Debra Manette came to the rescue and did an amazing job. She got me back on track and reenergized.

I am very excited about the artwork and style developed by illustrator, Fred Harper. Fred is well known for his caricatures and I was honored when he agreed to take on this project.

The friends and family who were there to support and encourage me along the way have been priceless. They have been great sounding boards and have given me insightful suggestions. Friends, such as the women from the Guacamole Club—Jane Wyszynski, Amy Bridgeman, and Catherine Lippman—have been bigger influences than they will ever know. Many other longtime friends—Dr. Joyce Braak, Carol Rutherford, Cathy Wiblemo, Phil Budahn, Gloria Smith, Pamela Porter, Pamela Thornton, Karen Walling, Patricia Crawford, Cyre Rodriguez, Claudia Tung, and Karen Laster Nusi, — have each inspired and believed in me along the way, even when I was a bit "out there" and stressed. My mom, Rachel Garrick, has always been my biggest fan no matter what I have done, my sister, Mary Sue, has found the love to tolerate me, Myron and Evelyn Garelick who have been such a find, and all of my cousins for their two cents. My former husband, Dennis Tenety, has always been good at supporting me even when I am sure he had no idea what I was talking about.

I am also grateful to those who have provided reviews for this book: Dr. Mike Magee, Brig. Gen. Wilma Vaught, USAF (Ret), Congresswoman Eddie Bernice Johnson (D-TX), Jen Hendershott, Matt Shepley, Murriel Page, and Sister Sledge. They are such consummate professionals that having their support is an honor. I am also grateful to those who actually have helped me lose the weight. Brian Dewey sold me my first gym membership at Fitness First and all of the trainers and instructors there answered a myriad of questions early on in my quest, especially Kate Berg, who taught me to appreciate yoga, and Mike Van Veen, who helped me rehabilitate my right knee after surgery. I am also grateful to all of the women at Wheaton Curves: the owners, Barbara Brenkworth and Lucia Mercer, the employees, and the clientele whose questions I hope I was able to answer. I wish I could remember the name of the Army doctor I saw at Walter Reed Army Medical Center who first diagnosed my high cholesterol and told me I could die. She probably saved my life. The best thing she did was to refer me to Primary Care at the Veterans' Affairs Medical Center in Washington, DC, where Dr. Becker and a dietitian taught me to rethink my relationship with food.

Finally, there are no words to express how deeply those veterans who have let me into their worlds and have shared so much of their fears and their dreams have touched me, especially "my boys" in New York (Frank Torres, Roland Bailey, John Lukasik and Mike and Janet Miller). They have given back more than they will ever know. They are our nations' veterans and my heroes.

Preface

I USED TO HATE IT when coworkers or other people I would meet at a party or the gym would tell me, "Oh, you can too!" after I had complimented them on how good they looked or was impressed by how much they jogged. Their optimistic declaration made me want to take my words right back. I was convinced that there was no way I could ever change my lifestyle. I could not see making diet and exercise such a focal point of my life, even though I was a healthcare professional. At restaurants, I watched as these skinny human-mutations pushed food around on their plates, took three bites, and then gave pasta primavera back to the waiter and said, "no" when he asked if they wanted a doggie bag! Hadn't anyone ever told them about the starving children in Africa or India? What was wrong with these people? Now, if you happen to be one of these people who are six feet tall, 110 pounds, think running is fun, and don't know what tofutti is, then this book is not for you. However, if you hate to diet, don't like to sweat, and have never tried to get your foot over your head in a yoga class, and then keep reading. I am talking to you. And the most annoying thing I am going to say is—get ready: *You can too!*

I decided to write this book after so many people began asking me how *I* lost 75 pounds. (I think people, especially the ones who knew me best, were shocked that I had found the willpower and desire actually to get off of my couch and eat tofu.) I've been collecting tips, clipping articles, reading research studies, and stashing brochures for over four years now and have kept the pounds off for that time period. Basically, what I discovered was that there were no quick-fix diet plans or easy exercise programs that would work. I needed to change my attitude and my lifestyle. So, *You Can Too* is more about healthy living rather than a (yet another) book about weight loss. This book is not a scientifically sound program that requires you to weigh food on a scale (*Who wants to bother with that!*) or engage in a repetitive exercise routine (unless that is what you want to do). Simply, this is my story, and the tips and good advice I found along the way that made me believe that I could live healthy and lose weight too, which turned out to be the most important thing.

Weight loss and weight management are as much a mental and spiritual exercise as they are a physical one. I had to change my approach to how I lived my life, not just to what I ate. I had to make a mind-body-spirit connection. I had to tackle my stressors and find the positive forces that would keep me motivated and inspired. I took my health risks into consideration and then designed a fitness and nutrition program that was right for me. I hope that by sharing my story and discoveries, you will have found a friend, as well as the inspiration and motivation to believe in yourself and know that you can too.

Introduction

THE "LAND OF THE FREE" is certainly not the land of the fat-free. In America today more and more adults are overweight, with our children increasingly catching up on the scales. According to the Centers for Disease Control, the number of obese adult Americans has risen by 60 percent since 1991. Today obesity affects approximately 60 percent (or two-thirds) of the population and 13 percent of our children. In 1970, obesity affected 47 percent of the population.

Adults are considered obese when they are approximately 30 pounds overweight or have a body mass index (BMI) of 30. In actuality, they are overweight with a BMI over 25. (For more information on BMI, see *Body Mass, Not Pounds* tip.) Obesity is a key factor in heart disease, diabetes, kidney and bladder disease, as well as some cancers, which are all on the rise in the United States. Excess weight affects the ability to breathe and puts strain on the heart, which results in premature death. Researchers have been able to show that individuals who are overweight in their 40s are more likely to die three years earlier than their slimmer counterparts. Obese people are likely to die five to seven years earlier. People suffering from obesity also suffer from joint and knee pain, which can lead to surgery and other medical treatments. Not to mention the stigma and emotional stress that affects people who are overweight in our thin-is-beautiful culture.

When I was in grade school in the 1970s, I remember just one girl in the entire suburban elementary school who was, well, fat. It was an oddity at that time, and I am sure she suffered greatly for it. But today, everywhere I go, I see teens and preteens walking around who are not just a bit flabby, but obese. This trend has been on the increase as more and more young people are playing indoors with Nintendo and Xboxes rather than out riding bikes and skipping rope. I remember when all of the children on my block used to meet in the middle of the street for Double Dutch, but I fear that most kids today would think that was some sort of pie. Electronic toys and concerns for safety have forced more children inside with less room to play, run, jump, or swing.

Meals in America have also changed. When I was growing up, McDonald's was for road trips and special treats, it was not part of a family's regular meal plan. Hamburgers and fries were a lot smaller than they are today. In fact, hamburgers have doubled in size from 4 ounces to 8 ounces, the fries have gone from 5 ounces to 7 ounces, and sodas have gone from 32 to 64 ounces. In general, portion sizes in America have increased by two to five times what they were 30 years ago, according to a study published in the *Journal of Public Health.* Super sizing our meals has led to a super sizing of our population. Americans in general are fatter than people are in most other countries, where smaller portions are the norm and physical activity has not changed as much. For example, the French diet is very high in fat, but not high in calories because the portion sizes are so much smaller. In America, we have more heart disease, stroke, and diabetes than in other parts of the world as well. For a country that seems so conscious of how we look and produces more supermodels and stars than most places, our general population does not reflect that same image.

Obesity has become a public health hazard in America far more insidious than smoking, yet it gets much less of our attention. The Department of Health and Human Services estimates that $117 billion is spent each year to treat the diseases related to obesity. Insurance programs will cover treatment for heart disease or diabetes, but few will cover the expenses associated with weight-gain prevention. Although some insurance plans will now cover the costs of a dietitian or medication, medical and health-related industries can do much more to react to the engorging of America.

Furthermore, on average, patients spend an additional $1,500 out of their own pockets in medical expenses when they are overweight. There are hidden costs of obesity for employers, as it contributes to employee absenteeism and work restrictions as a result of subsequent disease; nevertheless, very few insurers or employers offer beneficiaries preventive or weight-control options, such as assistance with health club membership or diet plans. (You may want to check with your insurer before seeing a primary care provider to learn what coverage options you can discuss during your appointment.) A positive example is Health Net, a managed care company that offers its employees a fitness center on site and reimburses them for their health club memberships at other locations (plus other amenities). It would be great to see more employers act this way. In my experiences as a health consultant with various organizations, I have seen that the better off employees are physically and mentally, the better their morale, productivity, and timeliness. When employers create healthy environments, which include fitness activities or walking clubs at lunchtime, management retreats, and fun activities, workers respond by being more dedicated to their corporate mission, establish stronger teams and take less days off.

Consumers also pay for other hidden costs related to obesity when it comes to designing and selling all kinds of products and services. Car manufacturers have researched creating roomier car seats that will accommodate larger drivers. Almost all food manufacturers' brands have created lines of low-fat, low-carbohydrate, sugar-free products. The travel and tourism industry has developed special tourist packages and hotels build rooms that accommodate larger guests. The cost for all of this research, development, and marketing gets passed along to consumers in the form of higher prices.

Even though obesity has public health and other societal ramifications, very little is being done to control the effects of unhealthy living. Few government programs or employee-based incentives are available to help. It would be great if there were more such programs available for Americans battling obesity and its related diseases. But, for now, making healthy living choices is up to you. Even though you are certainly not alone in battling the bulge in this country, you are the person with the primary responsibility to do something about it.

Not everyone needs (or wants) to look like Britney Spears, but certain habits and lifestyle choices will lead you to a healthier, fitter you. Be aware that there are traditional and popular cultural influences affecting your ability to make healthy lifestyle choices (consider Great-Grandma Maria's tiramisu recipe or the 99-cent offer to super size your fries). *You Can Too* will help you learn how to identify these temptations and teach you the techniques to avoid them in the future. Understanding the problem is the first step in being able to solve it. The next step is to develop a simple plan of attack that will work for you and can easily be incorporated into your lifestyle. Remember, this is not a diet that you will begin and end in a few weeks. This is about your life.

My Story

I CAN'T REMEMBER A TIME in my life when I didn't worry about my weight, but I never thought of it as having an impact on my longevity until an Army doctor told me I could die when I wasn't even 40 years old yet. Her matter-of-fact pronouncement regarding my obesity and a high cholesterol lab result got my attention and made me evaluate my lifestyle and my approach to food. Four years and 75 pounds later, I was fit enough to participate in the Bikini and Model Universe competitions sponsored by ESPN International. As I strutted across a camera lit stage over looking Miami Beach in a tiny red bikini, I realized that I had come a long way.

I never looked like the models in magazines. I was never athletic, but I have spent some time on and off over the years in aerobics classes and gyms. I grew up on Long Island with a health-conscious mother and a naturally skinny younger sister, but I took after my father's side of the family, where the big eaters and the big hips were. My mom has always fussed at me about my weight, yet she was the one who taught me to clean my plate in the first place, so it only seems fair to blame her whenever I gain a few pounds. I think this is in the unofficial mother/daughter rulebook under the sections, "You will be the death of me" and "It's all your fault—you raised me this way."

In high school and college, boys were the big motivator to look good. Some of the best times I can recall from those years are sitting on my friend Claudia's bed reading *Seventeen* magazine, watching *General Hospital*, and talking about boys. Big hair, designer jeans, and blue eye shadow were in vogue, and that is all we thought we needed to be happy and feel good. We lived for Friday or Saturday nights when we could sneak into the discos with our fake IDs (the drinking age was 18 in New York then, so I really am *that* old), dance the night away, oh, and of course, meet boys. When I graduated high school, I was 115 pounds and wearing a junior size 7 dress! Those were the days.

After that, I attended Nassau Community College for two years, earned an associate's degree, and lived at home. I kept some of the same friends, made new ones, and kept on going to the clubs. I spent a summer in Israel working on a kibbutz and came back with a great tan and in the best shape I had ever been.

I had gotten more serious about my studies and future plans when I went to Temple University in Philadelphia. I was dating a guy steadily and gained 20 pounds. I have since learned that this is a common phenomenon for students who first leave home and have to make their own food choices. College campuses are loaded with fast food restaurants, and late-night study snacks become a student's lifeline. I was no exception. Since college was also expensive, cheap carbo-loaded meals like pasta were a mainstay. Philadelphia also specializes in hoagies and cheese fries, which were a new taste sensation for this Long Island girl. While working with Vietnam combat veterans as a social work intern, I was driving an hour and a half each way from school in Philadelphia to the VA hospital in Coatesville, Pennsylvania. Sitting in the car three hours a day was not conducive to a healthy lifestyle, either. Today I can't imagine keeping those hours while still finding the time and energy to go to nightclubs (disco by now was dead).

After the boyfriend was long gone, I returned to New York with a master's degree in social work. For a few years I worked in an agency counseling Vietnam veterans and their families where I developed a specialization in treating posttraumatic stress disorder (PTSD). When I left that agency, I spent several months in the former Soviet Union consulting with veterans who had served in Afghanistan. I traveled extensively throughout Russia and the Ukraine, educating veterans about PTSD, which many suffered from due to their combat experiences. I was able to share with them the experiences of Vietnam veterans in America and spent many long hours discussing atrocities, abuse, grief, domestic violence, and alcoholism. At the time in Russia, I had little reason to worry about dieting since there was little edible food. Living conditions were difficult; the Soviet Union had recently collapsed, and the social structure of the country was in turmoil. My meals with former soldiers consisted of bread, broth, sardines, potatoes, cabbage, bottled water, and vodka. Yum. Thank goodness for the Fig Newton's that I had smuggled into the country in my suitcase. Not only did my trip make me horribly sick, it afforded me the opportunity to lose the pounds I needed to lose to meet the weight restriction to join the U.S. Army.

In July 1992, I accepted a commission to become a U.S. Army Officer, where physical fitness was part of the job. However, as a social work officer, it was not a big part of *my* job. I was stationed at Walter Reed Army Medical Center in Washington, DC, which did not call for traversing rugged treacherous terrain on a regular basis, unless you count the DC metro system. My patients kept me busy and I exercised when I could, but I did end up putting on a few pounds before I got out of the Army after three years. I stayed in Washington as a member of The American Legion national staff and lobbied for veterans' healthcare benefits.

One of the most important things I've learned about DC is that it is packed with fabulous restaurants, lobbyist receptions, and long working hours. Over the next five years, I gained 50 pounds. Thanks to the fashion designers, you can still be sharp-dressed in a size 16. So I kept going shopping (what an incentive!) and told myself I was enjoying my life and that gaining weight as you age is not uncommon. I had long ago stopped trying to look like the girls in the fashion magazines I loved in high school and was more concerned with the serious health policy issues that were affecting our nation's veterans. Yet without realizing it, I had put my own health at risk. (This is a great example of taking yourself too seriously for your own good.)

My wake-up call came on December 9, 2000. I had been recalled by the Army to take a physical exam for the 2290th Reserve unit. I still had three more years of an Army inactive reserve obligation to finish. By this time I had been out of the Army for five years and had slipped away from the exercise program that I had followed while on active duty. On the day of my recall exam, the attention getter was not so much my weight but my cholesterol, which had soared to 261, way over the 200 limit for a healthy level. A high level of cholesterol is a risk factor for heart disease, which is the number-one cause of death among American women. With my history of asthma, high cholesterol was not a good combination. I immediately followed up with my primary care provider and a dietitian at the local Veterans Affairs hospital. They provided a lot of great information on cholesterol-lowering diets and exercise. The goal was to try to get my cholesterol under control without the use of prescription medication, which I have so far been able to do. My most recent cholesterol reading was 161, and my primary care physician could not have made me feel better about what I had accomplished.

I had worked in the medical arena long enough to know that proper nutrition and physical activity were the key ingredients to getting my cholesterol problem under control. So, I dusted off the stationary bike in my bedroom and got back on it. Initially I could do only 15 minutes at a time, a few days a week, but now I can go for at least an hour, sometimes two! I am always looking for new activities to try: tennis, volkswalking (walking clubs that started in Europe), swimming, kickboxing, Pilates, and yoga—anything that gets me moving. Shopping, which in my family is a sport, has also been a great activity to keep me motivated and monitor my progress as I bought smaller and smaller sizes.

My family and friends, most of whom are health professionals, have been wonderful help. I have four great friends, and we have formed what we call the Guacamole Club. It acts as an unofficial support group for a bunch of overachieving, highly motivated, compassionate women who want true friends with whom they can share their dreams, frustrations, loves, and losses. They are the best! They have helped develop a lot of the tips that are discussed in the following pages. They have also gotten out there with me and played tennis, albeit very badly. (Laughing is also a great calorie burner!) They have been a great source of encouragement and motivation. One of the Guacamole Club members, Jane, bought me a tofu cookbook, and my Marine Corps–Retired, motorcycle-riding husband actually bought me my first box of tofu.

Since my primary goal was to lower my cholesterol without medication, diet was going to be more important than just a vigorous exercise program, and food took on a new significance. I have had to learn a great deal about serving sizes and saturated fats. Today I eat mostly fruits and vegetables, salad with salsa and lemon (not salad dressing), frozen low-fat yogurt, and egg whites. I use cooking spray and olive oil, and have come to know the joy of soy. Because life without chocolate just wouldn't be the same, I have made special allowances for certain occasions. Surprisingly, I have found that my body no longer craves the same fatty high-caloric foods that I was used to. When once only chocolate could save the day, now a banana seems to do the trick. At last count, my cholesterol was down 100 points and I had lost over 75 pounds, not a bad side effect. This has made a difference in other aspects of my life too. I am not as tired as I used to be and have more energy throughout the day. I breathe better and my complexion is brighter. I feel good about myself and look younger and sexier at 40 than I did at 30!

This experience has also made me want to share what I have learned with others. While working at The American Legion, I learned how to be an advocate for patient education and saw firsthand the difference it made when disabled veterans had the right information to make decisions and choices relevant to their healthcare. I wanted to be able to do more of that type of work, which is why I began saving the information I was collecting on healthy living to include in this book. The desire to educate healthcare consumers is also why it took the last bit of courage I had to leave the comforts of six years with The American Legion and start my own consulting business. I enjoyed the opportunity to work on some great projects, including a Curves franchise that allowed me to directly help other women face the issues of obesity and poor health. This experience motivated me to become a Certified Personal Trainer. I hope to be able to share my health and fitness experiences with an even broader audience.

All in all, I have learned that I needed to know more about my body, my spirit, and myself. Each area of the strong mind-body-spirit connection is an essential component in achieving healthy living success. For this reason, the tips I have developed go beyond just diet and exercise. If we want to improve our health and our habits, it is also important to change how we think and how we feel about our lives and ourselves. Otherwise, we fall back into old patterns, experiencing yo-yo weight loss and gain. I will always need to watch my cholesterol level and it would be nice to lose another five pounds, but I am confident that I have made the hardest changes and have learned new behaviors that will keep me going.

Your Story

BEFORE YOU CAN CHANGE your habits and behaviors, it helps to first take some time and think about your own story and experiences. Identifying the cause(s) of a problem is always the first step toward fixing it. You have to be able to see for yourself what factors have influenced your life, eating habits, and activity level. Journaling your own story is an important step in examining the traits that got you to a point in your life where you recognize that you are not living as healthfully as you should be. Start by using this section to think about your own history and influencing factors. You can use the space provided in this section of the book and record your answers here, use a separate journal, or you can go to the keyboard. The important thing to do here is to write your thoughts down. Regardless of how you choose to do this first step, be sure to answer the questions in the next section.

Write Down Your Own Story

- ? Think about how you have viewed your health and your body over the years. How has your view changed?
- ? What influences and key factors have played a part in your weight gain?
- ? What encouragements and motivations have helped you lose weight?
- ? What were your family attitudes about food while you were growing up?

- ? Who were your role models, and what were their eating habits?
- ? What (or who) sends you hightailing it to the nearest Ben & Jerry's or Starbucks? What stresses you out?
- ? What has helped you maintain a healthy body image in the past?
- ? What things can you do to improve your body image now?
- ? What are your future goals, not just for your body, but also for your life in general?
- ? What do you need to do to reach those goals? How does your body image affect your desire for success?

Next, focus on your healthy living goals. Be very specific about what you want to change. Use the following section to outline these goals once you have completed the previous section on documenting your own story and influences.

If I haven't been able to convince you to write out your life's story because you simply don't have the time for that, then at least list a few *realistic* healthy living goals regarding eating habits and weight loss.

LIST YOUR HEALTHY LIVING GOALS

I want to change these eating habits:

✔

✔

✔

✔

✔

(Add more space if needed.)

Weight-loss goals:

(Note: The gurus say that about one to two pounds a week is good.)

- ✔ **1 week:**
- ✔ **1 month:**
- ✔ **3 months:**
- ✔ **6 months:**
- ✔ **1 year:**
- ✔ **2nd year:**

Maintenance:

If you really want to engage in a long-term relationship with your scale, keep a calendar near it and log in your weight each week. Your weight will fluctuate daily, but over the course of several weeks, you should be able to track trends in your weight loss or gain. This can help you monitor your progress and be able to identify extraneous factors, such as water retention periods or outlier time periods, such as vacation weeks.

Tips

MY INTENTION for this book is to organize the tips and hints that have helped me reach my goals for a healthier life. I am not offering medical advice, although much of the material is based on my review of health literature and research studies. The statistical information comes from reliable sources, such as the Centers for Disease Control or the U.S. Department of Agriculture, not Aunt Sophia's Home Page. I have crosschecked information and have noted controversial issues as best as I can identify them. Ultimately, these tips are based on my own experience as one fat girl's yearning to be free who thought she could help others on a similar quest. Every "tell me what you did to look so great" conversation I have had with women at parties, while working at Curves, or at family gatherings has inspired me to want to share these tips. The one thing I know that works best in trying to achieve a healthier lifestyle is the support of the people around you.

The tips are meant to be easy to read and usable as quick references, because I know you are busy and don't have time for long, drawn-out explanations. I have also tried to be entertaining and funny, so laugh in the appropriate places, please.

I encourage you to come up with some of your own tips. Use a journal or the empty pages in this book to log in the things that have helped you and track your own progress. Good luck!

HEALTH TIPS

As I was making changes to my diet and exercise routine, I realized I needed to know more about how my body functioned. Since the thing that got me to think about all of this in the first place was cholesterol, I wanted to know more about it and how it could affect my health. In researching cholesterol, I discovered other information on the diseases related to obesity, such as heart disease and other health concerns for women, which were important factors in maintaining a healthy lifestyle for me as well. I needed to know how my weight was affecting everything from my breathing to my bones. It also became important to look at general health information, and I have included these issues in this first set of tips.

As a side note, although many of the tips are written with women in mind, there are important lessons here for men as well, because men as a group tend to pay less attention to medical conditions and their overall health. Male readers should be applauded and encouraged to focus in on their own gender-specific health issues and share information with their partners. If you can't get your man to read this book, that's OK, just arrange the doctor's appointment anyway. He'll complain, but he'll go to avoid a bigger argument. Oh, and go to the doctor with him, so someone can explain his health status without the macho airs and bravado. I mentioned I have had a husband, right? Enough said!

If you are diagnosed with a medical condition, it is very important that you tailor any diet and exercise program with your doctor's instructions and maintain medication compliance. If you have a family history or other risk factors for illnesses, such as diabetes or breast cancer, you should become familiar with healthful living habits that can reduce those factors. Review these tips and find out more about your own family history by talking to your mother, father, or older sibling who may know more about grandma's heart disease or grandpa's colon cancer. You should also talk to your in-laws to learn your partner's family health history. Your primary care provider will be interested in this information, I assure you.

It is important to know as much as you can about your body and your health before making any changes and to make sure that the changes you make are right for your age, gender, and health risks. You don't want to lose weight by depriving your body of necessary vitamins and minerals; nor do you want to begin an exercise routine that will leave you dehydrated or injured.

Eating Disorders Defined

Although I am going to concentrate on overweight and obesity problems, I feel it vital to address the issues surrounding anorexia nervosa and bulimia nervosa, two conditions described as eating disorders in the fourth edition of the *Diagnostic and Statistical Manual of Mental Disorders (DSM-IV)* published by the American Psychiatric Association. Anorexia and bulimia are serious mental health conditions that should not be associated with healthy or recommended approaches to weight loss. In fact, these conditions are life threatening. If you or anyone you know suffers from any of the following symptoms, seek immediate medical attention.

Anorexia nervosa is characterized by the refusal to maintain a minimally healthy body weight for age and height with an intense fear of gaining weight. Anorexics perceive themselves as fat even though they are underweight. These individuals will appear emaciated and gaunt.

Bulimia nervosa is diagnosed when a person repeatedly induces vomiting, uses laxatives, diuretics, drugs, excessive physical activity, and/or fasting after binge eating to prevent weight gain. Bingeing involves high-fat foods and sweets, which usually are consumed in large quantities. Bingeing and purging behavior becomes habitual over a prolonged period of time and is done secretly. Unlike people with anorexia, those with bulimia tend to keep their body weight at a minimally normal level.

People who have either of these disorders have a serious misperception of their body and overall self-image based on weight. The diseases are especially common among female teenagers. Anorexics and bulimics link their sense of self-worth to their bodies much more than other people and are in denial about their life-threatening malnourishment. They are susceptible to episodes of depression and anxiety, and often avoid social situations. As their weight drops below minimum levels necessary to maintain good health, these individuals, especially anorexics, are at serious risk for numerous medical conditions including cardiovascular and renal problems, osteoporosis, anemia, and dental problems. Starvation and malnourishment can be fatal.

Because anorexia and bulimia nervosa are serious mental and medical health threats, anyone suffering from them should seek professional help immediately. Specially designed inpatient and outpatient programs address these eating disorders. If you or someone you know is suffering from either of these conditions or already engaging in some binge/purge behavior, contact a primary care provider to get help in controlling these behaviors before they become life threatening. You can also check online for treatment resources and peer support. (See the list of Internet Resources.)

Obesity is *not* an eating disorder. In spite of all of the mass media and self-help attention paid to the psychological association among stress, self-esteem, and obesity, obesity is not characterized as a mental health disorder. Unlike anorexia and bulimia, there is not enough evidence linking obesity to a consistent psychological or behavioral syndrome. Obesity is, however, considered a general medical condition and is classified in the *International Classification of Diseases* handbook. Psychological factors or another diagnosis can influence a person's excessive weight gain, but obesity itself is not characterized in the *DSM-IV*.

Go to the Doctor

My story began with an eye-opening visit to a doctor, so I would have to recommend that you start there too. If you are concerned about your weight and health, consult with a primary care provider for a complete physical exam before doing anything else. There could be a medical reason for your weight gain, such as polycystic ovaries, a thyroid condition, edema, or a tumor. If you ignore symptoms, these conditions can become more hazardous to your health than your weight. Share your concerns with your primary care provider and get blood work done to check cholesterol, triglycerides, and glucose levels. These functions are an important part of your body's cardiovascular system and need to be at healthy levels. If you are nervous about seeing the doctor alone, bring a family member or a friend with you who can provide support and keep track of the information the doctor has given you. (In my experience, men should never be allowed to go to the doctor alone.) Don't be shy about asking for referrals and second opinions.

Use the *Doctor Visit Checklist* on the following page and don't be afraid to ask your doctor questions about your condition or share your concerns. Write out a list of questions before you go, so you can reference it quickly and have additional space to write down answers to help remember what the doctor told you. If something occurs to you after the visit, call the office and at least speak to a triage or advice-line nurse who might be able to help answer your questions. Don't just ignore a problem or decide it's not worth the trouble. It's your health; it's worth the trouble.

Several key factors affect your body's functioning, especially regarding weight gain and loss.

You need to know about:

Blood Pressure: *A healthy blood pressure for an adult is about 120 (systolic) over 80 (diastolic).* People diagnosed with high blood pressure, or *hypertension,* have had at least two readings above 140 over 90. High blood pressure causes the heart to work harder, which weakens it over time and can lead to heart attack or failure, stroke, or kidney failure. Obesity, smoking, elevated cholesterol, and diabetes are all risk factors that can lead to high blood pressure and cardiovascular disease.

Cholesterol: Cholesterol is a fatty, wax-like substance in your blood that your body needs to make cell membranes and hormones. However, too much cholesterol in your blood can build up inside arteries (arteriosclerosis) and block the flow of blood to your heart or brain, causing a heart attack or stroke, which is the most common cause of death among America women, especially African American and all postmenopausal women. Cholesterol has two parts. *Low-density lipoprotein*

(LDL), or what is otherwise called "bad," cholesterol is pretty self-explanatory. *High-density lipoprotein* (HDL), with the nickname "good" cholesterol, actually helps send extra cholesterol to your liver where it can be broken down, thereby reducing the risk for heart disease. *According to the National Heart, Lung and Blood Institute, you want your overall cholesterol level to be under 200, your LDL to be less than 130, and your HDL to be between 35 and 50.* Diet and exercise can help lower cholesterol, but not always, and you can be very thin and still have high cholesterol. Medications called *statins* help block the production of cholesterol in the liver and can lower levels by 30 to 50 percent. You will need your doctor to evaluate you before using these medicines since they are not available over the counter.

Triglycerides: These are another type of fat in your bloodstream similar to cholesterol. Triglycerides come from the foods you eat, especially carbohydrates, and are the body's main source of energy storage. Your triglyceride level should be below 200.

Glucose: This is the sugar found in the bloodstream, which fuels the body and will make you feel energetic. It is also a key factor in *diabetes.* The pancreas makes insulin that helps break down the sugar in our blood. If your body makes little or no insulin, then you are *insulin deficient* or have *type-1 diabetes.* If your body makes the insulin but your cells don't use it, then you are *insulin resistant* or have *type-2 diabetes.* According to the National Institutes of Health, *a normal blood sugar level is between 70 and 115 milligrams per deciliter (mg/dL).* You can become hypoglycemic when your blood sugar falls below 70 mg/dL or hyperglycemic if it goes above 120 mg/dL. Hypoglycemia is a condition not a disease that occurs when there is not enough sugar in the blood to fuel the body. This is can lead to an emergency situation if you are a diabetic rather than having just missed a meal or two. Hyperglycemia can become dangerous over time and can lead to tissue and nerve damage. A *fasting plasma glucose blood test* is a common test for diabetes. (Don't memorize this, just ask your doctor to check you for diabetes, especially if you are having some of the symptoms mentioned on the following page.)

As the rates of obesity have risen in America, so has the rate of diabetes. According to the Centers for Disease Control, studies have shown that obese adults can have a 93 percent risk for diabetes.

I have seen lots of great information on diabetes management. If you are diagnosed with diabetes, ask your doctor for diabetes management tool kits. The pharmaceutical companies that make some of the prescription medications for treating diabetes, such as Pfizer, Eli Lilly, and Takeda, produce tons of informative patient education materials. You can search their websites or call their toll-free lines and order booklets and videos from them if your provider does not have them available. My friend Jane, a nurse, gave me a great diabetes calendar book that had nutrition and exercise tips for each day; even though they were meant to control blood sugar, which isn't a problem for me, the tips were useful. This calendar book turned me on to all of the great free stuff you can get from the health and fitness industry. (See *Get Free Stuff* tip.)

SYMPTOMS OF DIABETES

- ✔ Increased hunger and thirst
- ✔ Tired and fatigued
- ✔ Irritability
- ✔ Dry, itchy skin
- ✔ Obesity
- ✔ Unexplained weight loss (not always a good thing!)
- ✔ High blood pressure
- ✔ Slow-healing wounds and infections of the skin, gums, or bladder
- ✔ Sexual problems, especially erectile dysfunction for men
- ✔ Vaginitis or yeast infections in women
- ✔ Increased urination, especially at night
- ✔ Numbness or tingling in feet or hands
- ✔ Blurred vision
- ✔ Family history

Body Mass Index (BMI): This is simply a formula that compares your height and weight and can also help determine your health risks. The National Institutes of Health's National Heart, Blood and Lung Institute determined that a healthy BMI is between 19 and 24. However, to avoid heart disease, your BMI should be under 22; to reduce your diabetes risk, it should be under 28; for cholesterol lowering and to help avoid breast cancer, it should be under 27.

Use the BMI chart in the next section to calculate your own BMI and set a new goal. Many health professionals, such as primary care providers and dietitians, today feel this number is more indicative of your health than pounds on the scale.

Bone Density: As we age, we may develop osteoporosis, a disease that causes our bones to become more porous, brittle, and susceptible to fractures. (The problem is especially common among postmenopausal women.) Calcium, magnesium, and Vitamin D are important factors in preventing osteoporosis, but it is a good idea to ask about a ***bone density check*** when you visit your primary care provider, especially if you are over the age of 50 and/or are menopausal, a smoker, have a family history of osteoporosis, have used steroids continually, or are Asian or Caucasian. You may also want to ask for this test if you have notice a curvature in your spine, height loss (are your pants suddenly too long?), or unexplainable severe back pain.

See a Dietitian

Your primary care provider can refer you to a Registered Dietitian, if need be or if you would like someone to work with you. A Registered Dietitian is credentialed by the American Dietetic Association (ADA); has achieved a bachelor's degree, participated in an accredited supervised practice program, passed an exam administered by the Commission on Dietetic Registration; and undertakes continuing education courses to maintain his or her registration. A dietitian can tell you about your BMI and appropriate weight for your height and age as well as develop a comprehensive meal plan that is right for you. He or she will work with you over the long term and can be called on when you have questions or concerns. Dietitians are a great source of information and can keep you up to date on the latest research and products that can help you. They can teach you more about portion/serving size and how and which calories to count depending on your body's needs. If you already have high cholesterol, diabetes, or some other diagnosis, there are special issues to consider before beginning a new meal program. A dietitian can help you select a plan that will address those disorders. Dietitians may specialize in certain areas, such as maternal health, cancer care, or pediatrics. There are many commercial meal plans on the market today, such as Atkins, Weight Watchers, Jenny Craig, the Zone Diet, South Beach, The Curves Weight Loss Plan, and so on. A dietitian can review the pros and cons of these meal plans with you and select one that is best for you. For the most part, no matter what diet or meal plan you follow, you will lose weight as long as you are restricting calories and controlling portions. The challenge becomes making the lifestyle changes that you can maintain over the long term and what is best for your body's needs. A dietitian can help you sort out what your body needs if you are not sure about what to do.

It is important to note that there is a difference between a Registered Dietitian and a *Nutritionist.* A nutritionist's training is more limited and he or she may know about only certain types of programs or diets. For example, a nutritionist may be able to advise you on an organic diet designed to reduce the symptoms of menopause, but may not necessarily be trained on metabolic disorders. There may also be differences in fees and insurance coverage, so check it out and ask for credentials. Some insurance plans will cover the cost of a Registered Dietitian, but not a nutritionist. The ADA can help you find a Registered Dietitian in your zip code; visit the ADA at *www.EatRight.org* or call 1-800-877-1600.

I would strongly recommend that you do visit a Registered Dietitian for at least one consultation before going on any type of diet. There is a lot of information out there and some of it is wrong, so check things out with someone who is trained in nutrition and can guide you through the diet process.

Get Free Stuff (Including Medication)

Doctors' offices have great *free* stuff that they can give you. Pharmaceutical companies print this stuff up and ship it out by the truckloads. Pharmaceutical company representatives give doctors, clinics, hospitals, and pharmacies all kinds of great little guidebooks and diaries in which you can read all about weight loss and the diseases related to obesity, track your eating habits, and find healthy recipes and all kinds of other information on products and calories. I've also gotten foam stress balls, which you can squeeze to relieve tension, pill cases to help manage medication and improve compliance, and other fun stuff, such as travel bags, key chains, coffee mugs, and even a watch. I just love these things! Did I mention they were free? Besides, they are quick and easy to reference. For example, a Wellness Map brochure I have opens up to a poster and has all kinds of information on cholesterol control. I hung it up on the inside of my pantry door for easy access.

I have found all sorts of recipes in these materials that are great and easy to prepare. Many are disease specific, so if you are trying to lower your cholesterol or control diabetes, then look for these types of materials.

The information I have gotten for free has helped me to understand healthy eating and weight loss, so I could make the changes I needed to make in my life. There are also wallet-size calorie counters and other easy-to-read items that you can keep in a purse or a desk drawer for quick referral.

Also, remember to follow up every three to six months with your primary care provider or dietitian. Your doctor might have gotten new freebies, and you don't want to miss out. You also might want to check on your progress and discuss further changes in your health status while you are there. Don't be embarrassed to ask your physician for any materials, handouts, fact sheets, or pamphlets he or she may have. If they do not have materials to give you, research it yourself. If you are on any medication, find out who the manufacturer is and contact that company for patient education materials. Manufacturers offer everything from fact sheets to videos on certain diseases and their management.

Another alternative for free information are the associations—American Heart Association, American Lung Association, American Dietetic Association among many others. These associations produce materials that are disease specific and include nutritional care. Then there is always the federal government. Check with the Centers for Disease Control, National Institute of Health, Food and Drug Administration (FDA), Health and Human Services, Agriculture Department, and with Veterans Affairs (VA) if you are a veteran. I received most of my information from VA, and they are a known leader in the health research and development field. This information is also more likely to be objective and comprehensive than that offered by drug companies, because federal agencies are not selling a product or promoting a cause. You have paid your taxes, so you might as well get something out of the money you gave the feds: Get information from them!

Medication Can Be Discounted or Free Too!

A huge problem in America today is the number of uninsured people who cannot afford health care or medications. Life-saving medications can be expensive, but don't skip filling prescriptions because of the cost. If you are prescribed a medication you cannot afford, you may be able to get assistance directly from the pharmaceutical companies depending on your income and age. For example, Pfizer offers certain uninsured customers discounts on prescriptions. Most other drug companies offer similar programs. Call the toll-free number or visit the company website of the manufacturer of the drug you have been prescribed and see what discounts or assistance are offered.

Some civic organizations also offer discount prescription drug programs that could help defray the costs of medication. For example, if you are a member of the American Legion or the Auxiliary, you are eligible to participate in their RX America prescription drug discount benefit at participating pharmacies. You should check with any organizations or associations that you belong to and find out if they offer a similar discount program to their members.

Doctor Visit Checklist

Clip or copy the following page and take it with you to your next primary care appointment. Keep track of the dates of your office visits and blood levels checks so that you can compare them over time. Think of these visits in comparison to taking your car for an oil change. Because you have tracked your mileage each time you fill up at the gas station, you know when the car is due for an oil change. When the gas station finishes changing your oil, the mechanic adheres a little sticker on the inside of your car window telling you when the next oil change is due, and you keep track of that. So, you know to check your car's levels and keep records, so why not do the same thing with your own body? Isn't your heart as important as your car's transmission?

You *are the best expert on managing your own health.* You may notice changes in your blood test results over time or with your general health before your doctor, especially if you have been seen by numerous providers or have switched insurance plans. If your medical records are not electronic, how can you be sure your new provider has all the necessary information on your medical history prior to treating you? Keep your own records and documents. Know the names of your medications and dosages, so you can report them at an office visit or in the emergency room. Know what tests or X-rays you have had and where they are stored.

A visit to the doctor's office is also a good time to check your height and weight and discuss any changes. Remember that changes in weight or height can be indicative of other medical conditions or diseases, such as osteoporosis or a thyroid condition. Keep track yourself and share your log with your provider.

DOCTOR VISIT CHECKLIST

What is my

Blood Pressure:

Total Cholesterol: HDL: LDL:

Triglycerides:

Glucose:

Body Mass Index:

Weight:

Bone Density:

Height:

Last Pap Smear:

Last Mammogram:

Medication(s) & Supplements:

Date of Exam: ______________________________

Provider: ______________________________

Cancer Screening Checklist

While you are visiting the doctor, it is a good idea to screen for the cancers that most often affect women, which are *breast, lung, colorectal, endometrial, ovarian,* and *cervical.* You should get a *mammogram* every other year if you are a woman over 40 years of age and yearly after the age of 50. If you get a baseline mammogram when you are 40, changes in your breast tissue can be easier to detect, especially if you have genetic or other cancer risk factors (smoking, breast abnormalities, early menstruation, late menopause, used birth control pills or hormone replacement therapy for more than 10 years, and/or never had children; being overweight increases your chances for breast cancer by almost 20 percent, especially after menopause according to the Nurses' Health Study).

You should also perform monthly *breast cancer self-exams.* There is plenty of free stuff on this too, especially from the Susan G. Komen Breast Cancer Foundation (www.komen.org). The Komen Foundation prints self-exam cards that describe how to check your breasts while lying down, in front of a mirror, or in the shower. According to the Komen Foundation, to do a breast self-exam, you should use the pads of your fingers and in an up-and-down pattern make small circles over each breast. Use light, medium, and firm pressure, then gently squeeze the nipple for any discharge.

Make sure to schedule an annual *gynecological exam and Pap test* to determine any changes in your cervix or ovaries. Your weight gain may be the result of a tumor. I knew a woman who was overweight, but was also carrying around a 20-pound tumor! Tumors can be benign (not life-threatening) or malignant (cancerous) and deadly if left to grow untreated. But if caught in their early stages, many tumors can be very treatable. So get checked!

You should also be checked for *colorectal cancer.* There is an easier self-test kit available that you may want to start with if you are not as brave as Katie Couric, who had a well-publicized colonoscopy (a visual exam of the colon using a fiber optic scope). Ask your doctor more about the self-test kit and the exam.

MEN: If You Are Reading This (or If There Is a Man in Your Life)

You also need regular exams to check for colon, testicular, and prostate cancer, especially if you are over the age of 50. *Erectile dysfunction* can be a symptom of prostate cancer or diabetes, so go to the doctor if that is a problem too! Erectile dysfunction can be treated through medical intervention and prescription medication.

Just as women are advised by their doctors to check for breast cancer, men should also perform self-exams for testicular cancer. Do this after a shower and while standing naked in front of a mirror. Check each testicle for a pea-size lump using both hands. Additional information on testicular cancer can be found online through the Testicular Cancer Resource Center. (www.tcrc.acor.org)

Quit Smoking

This probably does not require a big lecture. By this time, we all know the dangers of smoking and secondhand smoke. (I am including secondhand smoke as a weight issue because studies have shown that women who live with smokers tend to pick up on the poorer eating habits of the smoker and are more likely to be overweight.) But the reason I choose to address smoking here is that I have heard many women (and men for that matter) say that they can't give up smoking because of all of the weight they would gain if they did. Although I was never a smoker myself, I have worked long enough in the healthcare arena to see many people give up smoking and not turn into a Macy's Thanksgiving Day Parade balloon. The fear of weight gain is based more on the psychological side effect of the addictive quality of the nicotine than on fact. It becomes the excuse not to try to change your lifestyle to a healthier set of behaviors. Smoking also impedes the flow of oxygen in your body and can make even the slightest exercise seem that much more exerting, which causes you to be even more sedentary and gain more weight. But fear not! I'm going to offer tips for smoking cessation too!

These are several tips that can help smokers quit:

- ✔ Consult your primary care provider for medication and counseling referrals.
- ✔ Join a support group for smokers.
- ✔ Find something else to do with your hands (i.e.: crochet, squeeze a ball).
- ✔ Chew sugarless gum.
- ✔ Have your clothes dry-cleaned or washed to rid them of the cigarette smell.
- ✔ Use the exercise, journaling, and relaxation tips in other sections of this book to get your mind off smoking.
- ✔ Visit association websites, such as that of the American Lung Association, and obtain other materials that can help you quit.

Nonsmokers Living with Smokers

If you are not a smoker but live with one or work with many, first, be kind. Smoking is an addiction, but you do not have to subject yourself to the smoke. Set agreed limits to where smoking can take place, such as the den, basement, garage, or outdoor porch. Secondhand smoke affects your body's ability to circulate oxygen too, and you don't want your circulation impeded, especially if you are trying to become more physically active. Use smoke-eater machines and air purification systems in your home if there is indoor smoking going on. My husband smokes in designated areas of the house (mostly the basement or outdoors), but having a smoke-eater machine, which sucks in the smoke has helped keep it from circulating throughout the house. I would love for him to quit, but so far, I have not been that lucky, but not for a lack of trying, I assure you!

Additionally, do not eat what the smoker eats. Think about that study I mentioned earlier and avoid the high-fat snacks smokers tend to crave. My husband would live on potato chips, but as far as I am concerned, chip bags should come with skulls and crossbones on them.

Body Mass, Not Pounds

If you're like me, you have never believed your bathroom scale to be an honest interpreter of your weight, and you are probably right. A better way of gauging your weight is to calculate your body mass index (BMI), which you can do using the table on the next page developed by the National Institutes of Health's National Heart, Blood and Lung Institute. You can also visit their website at *www.nhblisupport.com.*

A normal BMI range is between 19 and 24. Twenty-five to 29 is overweight and 30 to 39 is obese; anything over is extreme obesity. To determine your BMI, look at your height and your current weight. Then look for your ideal range in order to better understand how many pounds you need to lose to reach healthy weight. For example, if you are 5 foot 3 inches (63 inches tall) and weigh 190 pounds, your BMI would be 34, which would make you obese. To have a healthy BMI of at least 24, you should weigh 135 pounds. Therefore, you would need to lose 55 pounds to be healthier and to reduce your risks for the diseases related to obesity.

BODY MASS INDEX TABLE

To use the table, find the appropriate height in the left-hand column labeled Height. Move across to a given weight. The number at the top of the column is the BMI at that height and weight. Pounds have been rounded off.

BMI	19	20	21	22	23	24	25	26
Height (inches)	Body Weight (pounds)							
58	91	96	100	105	110	115	119	124
59	94	99	104	109	114	119	124	128
60	97	102	107	112	118	123	128	133
61	100	106	111	116	122	127	132	137
62	104	109	115	120	126	131	136	142
63	107	113	118	124	130	135	141	146
64	110	116	122	128	134	140	145	151
65	114	120	126	132	138	144	150	156
66	118	124	130	136	142	148	155	161
67	121	127	134	140	146	153	159	166
68	125	131	138	144	151	158	164	171
69	128	135	142	149	155	162	169	176
70	132	139	146	153	160	167	174	181
71	136	143	150	157	165	172	179	186
72	140	147	154	162	169	177	184	191
73	144	151	159	166	174	182	189	197
74	148	155	163	171	179	186	194	202
75	152	160	168	176	184	192	200	208
76	156	164	172	180	189	197	205	213

Source: *The National Institutes of Health, National Heart, Blood and Lung Institute*

BODY MASS INDEX TABLE (CONTINUED)

27	28	29	30	31	32	33	34	35
Body Weight (pounds)								
129	134	138	143	148	153	158	162	167
133	138	143	148	153	158	163	168	173
138	143	148	153	158	163	168	174	179
143	148	153	158	164	169	174	180	185
147	153	158	164	169	175	180	186	191
152	158	163	169	175	180	186	191	197
157	163	169	174	180	186	192	197	204
162	168	174	180	186	192	198	204	210
167	173	179	186	192	198	204	210	216
172	178	185	191	198	204	211	217	223
177	184	190	197	203	210	216	223	230
182	189	196	203	209	216	223	230	236
188	195	202	209	216	222	229	236	243
193	200	208	215	222	229	236	243	250
199	206	213	221	228	235	242	250	258
204	212	219	227	235	242	250	257	265
210	218	225	233	241	249	256	264	272
216	224	232	240	248	256	264	272	279
221	230	238	246	254	263	271	279	287

Know Thyself

Can you tell your glutes from your abs? It helps to know the muscle groups you need to exercise to improve your strength and tone. You also don't want to be lifting your laterals over your head when the exercise instructor calls for a biceps stretch. Think Schwarzenegger without his shirt (mmm) to help you visualize these muscle groups.

Key Muscle Groups to Know:

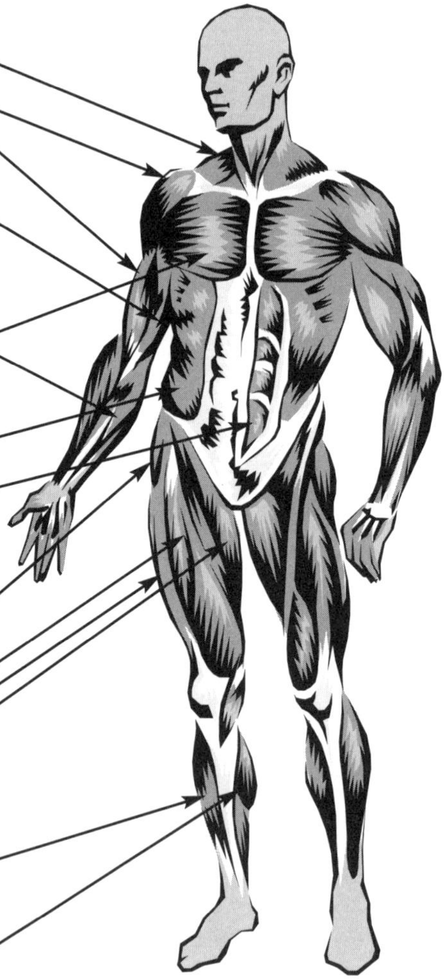

Avoid the "No Pain, No Gain" Theory

The "no pain, no gain" advice actually makes no sense at all. Those oversized, muscle-bound idiots who have something to prove to the rest of us usually espouse it. I was appalled when I saw a Bally's Fitness Center commercial pushing "beautiful pain" as a sales pitch to join their gym. Shameful, or should I say, idiotic!

Obviously, you will feel some muscle aches after you first begin to use parts of your body you didn't know you had. These aches can be best treated with ice. A package of frozen peas or corn works nicely here. You can also use over-the-counter sports creams or aspirin, and you should feel better in a few days. But if you are limping, can't stand up straight, or if blood is involved and pain persists for more than several days—this is advice men need to hear more often—then go to a doctor *before* body parts need to be reassembled. Don't try to "work it out" yourself by trying different stretches. Pain is our body's early warning alert system. It tells our brain that there is something wrong and that something needs to be done about it. If you have overly stressed or strained a muscle or fractured a bone, you need to see a qualified medical professional, not the buff rodent exterminator who is always at your gym. See your primary care provider or a chiropractor to deal with pain.

If you have had a previous back, knee, or other injury, talk to a Certified Personal Trainer (CPT) who can help you learn exercises that are better for you and can help you avoid another injury or can help strengthen problem areas. There are definitely exercises or yoga poses you should avoid if you have had a previous injury, if you have high blood pressure, or if you are pregnant.

FOOD TIPS

The most challenging part in changing my lifestyle was changing my relationship with food and what and how much I ate. I love food, and finding the right choices and healthy substitutes for my favorites took a bit of experimentation. I had to rethink my relationship with food to consider it as the fuel my body needs to function, not as a means of emotional gratification, which is why the previous set of health tips were important. The general health and nutrition information I collected helped me to understand how my body uses food and what it does and does not need as fuel to optimize my energy level and improve my fitness—and, oh yeah, I did lose weight! Trying new things and figuring out how to replace high-fat-calorie items with more nutritious choices actually has been fun. The substitutions I have listed on the following pages have been extremely helpful and a key factor in my weight loss. I have also had to work at controlling portion size, which admittedly was a bit harder for me. I have tackled portion size by loading up on the veggies first, which I can eat more of and do fill me up.

Although my mother always used to tell me not to play with my food, that is exactly what I have needed to learn how to do. To make foods more palatable to me, I have played with them by dressing them up and adding spices. I have experimented with all kinds of vegetables and combinations thereof. I have always enjoyed eating, but now I even enjoy the planning and preparation part more. I feel proud when I have concocted a new low-calorie meal that tastes great. Food is still fun, but now in a more goal-oriented way.

The following tips are meant to inspire and help you find some of the shortcuts I have discovered to improve my eating habits. Try to figure out some of your own tips too to suit your taste buds.

You Are What You Eat

My mom used to say, "You are what you eat" when I was growing up, and I used to make faces and mimic her when she wasn't looking. But there is a lot of truth in the statement. If you eat food that is high in fats …

well, you know the rest. It is more important to find a balanced diet that is part of your lifestyle than to go on a diet for short periods of time, which can lead to rebound weight gain or *yo-yo dieting*. In yo-yo dieting, you spend decades gaining and losing the same 10 pounds until you just give up altogether. By the next decade, you have gained 20 pounds. I have avoided the latest trends and fad diets and concentrated on building a healthy lifestyle approach to eating. My advice here is to go back to what Mother and your kindergarten teacher taught you.

MyPyramid • The New Food Pyramid

Grains

- ✔ Make half your grains whole
- ✔ Eat at least 3 oz. of wholegrain cereals, breads, crackers, rice, or pasta every day
- ✔ 1 oz. is about 1 slice of bread, about I cup of breakfast cereal, or 1/2 cup of cooked rice, cereal, or pasta

Vegetables

- ✔ Vary your veggies
- ✔ Eat more dark-green veggies like broccoli, spinach, and other dark leafy greens
- ✔ Eat more orange vegetables like carrots and sweetpotatoes
- ✔ Eat more dry beans and peas like pinto beans, kidney beans, and lentils

Fruits

- ✔ Focus on fruits
- ✔ Eat a variety of fruit
- ✔ Choose fresh, frozen, canned, or dried fruit
- ✔ Go easy on fruit juices

Milk

- ✔ Get your calcium-rich foods
- ✔ Go low-fat or fat-free when you choose milk, yogurt, and other milk products if you don't or can't consume milk, choose lactose-free products or other calcium sources such as fortified foods and beverages

Meat & Beans

- ✔ Go lean with protein
- ✔ Choose low-fat or lean meats and poultry
- ✔ Bake it, broil it, or grill it
- ✔ Vary your protein routine—choose more fish, beans, peas, nuts, and seeds

Find your balance between food and physical activity

- ✔ Be sure to stay within your daily calorie needs.
- ✔ Be physically active for at least 30 minutes most days of the week.
- ✔ About 60 minutes a day of physical activity may be needed to prevent weight gain.
- ✔ For sustaining weight loss, at least 60 to 90 minutes a day of physical activity may be required.
- ✔ Children and teenagers should be physically active for 60 minutes every day, or most days.

Know the limits on fats, sugars, and salt (sodium)

- ✔ Make most of your fat sources from fish, nuts, and vegetable oils.
- ✔ Limit solid fats like butter, margarine, shortening, and lard, as well as foods that contain these.
- ✔ Check the Nutrition Facts label to keep saturated fats, trans fats, and sodium low.
- ✔ Choose food and beverages low in added sugars. Added sugars contribute calories with few, if any, nutrients.

The U.S. Department of Agriculture updated its Food Guide Pyramid in 2005 for the first time since 1992. The new food guidance system, referred to as MyPyramid, places greater emphasis on personalization of nutritional choices. The four tiers of the old pyramid have been replaced with six bands representing 6 ounces of grains, 2-1/2 cups of vegetables, 2 cups of fruit, minimal use of oils, 3 cups of milk or other dairy, and 5-1/2 ounces of meat and/or beans. Foods from each of those sources are needed for a 2,000-calorie diet everyday. However, the width of the bands and narrowing of each section is a reminder to control portions and eat in moderation. The wider bands are the foods you should eat more of and the narrower ones are the food to control intake. The guy climbing the steps alongside is not a tomb-raider, but a reminder that no matter what you eat, physical activity is an important component of healthy living. For more detailed information on MyPyramid, go to the USDA website at www.mypyramid.gov. From the website you can use the MyPyramid Plan function to tailor the guidelines based on ur age, gender, and activity level. The site also has information for children.

Overall, you should know some of the basic food sources the your body needs, and the serving sizes it requires. You should be familiar with:

- ✔ **Carbohydrates:** Any type of foods that are sugars, starches, and cellulose. These are breads, cereals, pasta, rice, and grains. As your body metabolizes carbohydrates, they turn into glucose (sugar) in your blood stream. If you are very physically active, you will burn carbs first, which is why you may hear about athletes who carbo-load before a big race. You don't need to do this unless your fitness plan is vigorous.

- ✔ **Fats:** Any soft or solid organic compounds that contain glyceride esters of fatty acids and other related compounds. Fat is energy stored in the body and keeps us insulated. We need it, but often get too much, which leads to weight gain and high cholesterol. For more of a discussion on fat, see the *Fat Free* tip.
- ✔ **Fiber:** Those enzymes found in certain plants that aid in digestion make up soluble fiber. Fiber can be found in oats, beans, barley, and certain fruits (apples, pears, oranges, prunes). A high-fiber diet is believed to cut cholesterol and clean the colon.
- ✔ **Proteins:** Any complex nitrogen-based organic compounds that contain amino acids that exist in all living matter and are essential for tissue growth and repair. Our bodies need proteins. Most people get their protein from meat, chicken, dairy, or eggs but we can cut back on those higher-fat/cholesterol sources by also getting protein from fish, soy, beans, and nuts.
- ✔ **Vitamins:** Any of a variety of complex organic substances occurring naturally in the metabolic process of plants or animals. Nutritional research has documented recommended vitamin intake for human health. (See the tip on the *Vitamin Debate.*)

Fat Free

It should have been a Twinkie in the Garden of Eden instead of an apple since it's the fat in foods that makes them the most tempting. Reducing "bad fats" in your diet is key to weight loss and to lowering your cholesterol level. Some fats are not as bad as others, and we do need some fat in our diet, such as the fat found in salmon, nuts, and avocados. Fats are found in all dairy products, even in those that are low fat. All oils are 100 percent fat. One tablespoon of fat can have 120 calories, which can take you about a half hour to burn during a low-intensity cardio workout.

There are four types of fats:

- ✔ **Saturated fats.** They are solid at room temperature and come mostly from animals and tropical oils, such as coconut or coca butter and hydrogenated vegetable oil. This group of fats is the worst for you because these fats are the ones that increase your LDL, or "bad," cholesterol.

- ✔ **Polyunsaturated fats.** These are the fats that are liquid at room temperature and are found in vegetable oils. These fats can help reduce cholesterol.
- ✔ **Monounsaturated fats.** These oils are also liquid at room temperature and are actually linked to lowering LDL cholesterol levels. The two to use are olive and canola oils. (I prefer olive because it tastes better to me. I use mostly cooking spray and then some olive oil to add flavor.)
- ✔ **Hydrogenated fats.** These fats become hard and even more saturated at room temperature and are found in shortening, margarine, and nut butters. Lots of cakes, cookies, and crackers are made with these fats, so watch out for them because this stuff is the absolute worst for you. (Think about just how yucky it would be to walk around covered in goopy Crisco or just imagine how it would look pumped in under your skin; that should keep you from eating the stuff.)

  When you are in the supermarket, you really need to read the labels. The words *partially hydrogenated* should send you running for your life. (See *Supermarket Zone—Buyer Beware* tip for more on label reading.)

Your total daily caloric intake from fat should be 30 percent or less, depending on your cholesterol level and your desired weight-loss goal. To keep things simple, look for products that have 3 grams or less of fat per 100 calories. Avoid products that give you that amount of fat in one or two servings, especially if 3 crackers is a serving. I don't know about you, but, for me, 3 crackers are not worth the calories; they've never filled me up or made that much of a difference in soup to warrant that much fat. Make sure all of your dairy products are low-fat as well and select the soymilk when you can. Also know that there are low-fat soy (tofu or bean curd) products.

For Carb Counters

If you are more concerned about carbohydrates than fat, you should limit your carbohydrates to 20 grams per day. If you are not counting your carbohydrates, you still should not have more than 60 grams in a single day.

Portion Proportions

Moses may have been the first dietician. During the Exodus from Egypt, he instructed the Israelites to gather as much as they needed of the bread God had provided, and in the end, "He who had gathered much had no excess, and he who had gathered little had no deficiency: they had gathered as much as they needed to eat." (Exodus 16:10–18) The biblical lesson that applies to our lives today is to know when enough is enough. Portion size counts and will depend on your body's metabolism, your level of activity and nutritional value.

I know I said you would not have to measure out food to use this guide, but you should become familiar with portion size. My Eastern European–born grandmother had an amazing ability to pour salt into her hand while making stuffed cabbage that was "to die for" and be right on the money when it came to measuring a teaspoon. Her kitchen always smelled delicious, but there was not a measuring cup or spoons to be found. She instinctively knew how a finished dish needed to look, its consistency and its quantity, for it to come out perfect each time. Being able to visualize portions or serving sizes is similar to my grandma's cooking technique; you have to be able to recognize when enough is just right. If you read the labels that come on packaged foods, there is always a section that tells you how many calories are in a serving size, which is usually the recommended portion. But take heed! A candy bar label may list 120 calories, but the bar may be 2.5 servings, so you've consumed 300 calories.

Counting *calories* is important because energy is stored in our bodies in the form of fat. This energy is measured in calories. *Metabolism* is the process by which cells break down molecules to release this energy and heat. Hormones affect the metabolic rate and will vary depending on your genetics, age, gender, and body type. Unused energy (calories) is stored in the body as fat. Simply, if you burn more energy than you take in, you will lose weight. Just sitting in a chair and breathing burns calories. But the more cardio exercise you are doing, the more calories you will burn and the more fat you will lose, even when you are not exercising, because you will have sped up your metabolism. *You need to burn about 3,500 calories to lose 1 pound.* A daily diet should consist of *1,200 to 2,000 calories,* but the exact amount will depend on your level of activity and amount of weight you need to lose. Researchers have found that many obese Americans are consuming 5,000 calories daily. *(Oh my God!)* Therefore, the less active you are, the fewer calories you should take in. If I know I am going to kickboxing later on in the day, then I'll have pasta for lunch, because I will soon be burning off the carbohydrate calories. If I'm weightlifting it is a good day for protein.

The quickest way to cut calories and still enjoy your favorite foods is just to eat less of them. You can accomplish this by serving yourself your plate and putting leftovers away before eating or by taking extras to the nice old lady next door. You can also prepare meals and then portion them out and store them individually, so when you are ready to eat, you only have to warm up the one serving. You can do this with snacks too, so that the entire box of cupcakes will not tempt you, even if they are the low-fat variety.

Because we are used to having our meals super sized in America and restaurants serve mammoth portions to justify their exorbitant prices, we need to retrain our brain to recognize a full plate when it sees one. I made this task easier on myself by buying smaller plates. (Seriously, I went from 9-inch plates to 8-inch ones.)

I am also a glutton for seconds, so I serve myself less the first time in order to be able to get to have another serving. I'm lucky that I'm so gullible. But these small behavioral changes have helped. I also prepare lots of vegetables so I can fill up on them first. If you reduce the amount of high-fat foods and carbohydrates on your plate, you can still indulge in them. Go back to the food pyramid and become acquainted with the serving sizes for each of the food groups. Just remember that moderation is the rule.

P.S.: When eating at home, women should not serve themselves as much as the men at their table. Men have more muscle mass and can burn the extra calories quicker. Children should be served even less. If your entire family is fighting the battle of the bulge, then adjust everyone's—even the dog's—portions accordingly.

SERVING SIZES

1 serving of meat = 2-3 ounces cooked, (about the size of your fist)

1 serving of pasta or rice = 1 cup (about the size of a baseball)

1 serving of bread = 1 slice

1 serving of milk or yogurt = 1 cup

1 serving of cheese = 4 dice-size cubes

Remember: *labels on packaged food will tell you what a serving size for that product should be. This is important to pay attention to since a serving may only be 1 cup on one product, but 1/2 cup on another for the same amount of calories.*

Substitute, Don't Starve

The thing I have always hated about diets is the counting calories and weighing food. *Who the hell wants to do that*? I like to eat and want to enjoy it! Say it with me: "I like to eat and want to enjoy it!" For this reason, I was apprehensive about going to see a dietitian when my doctor first suggested it. However, when I finally did see a dietitian, she told me I should eat *six* smaller meals throughout the day, not just three big ones. Now, that was the good news, and I liked her immediately. The better news was that there were many things I did like to eat, but had not thought of them as foods I could use in other ways. For example, I love salsa, which has very little calories, but always just dipped my nachos in it. Now, I use it over salad and on a baked potato instead of high calorie dressings or sour cream.

Starving yourself for a few weeks won't help you lose weight permanently. It will just leave you dehydrated, undernourished, and susceptible to illness. By starving yourself, you might fit into the strapless dress you bought a size too small for your cousin Sally's wedding, but when you get there you will feel too sluggish to dance with the hunk she invited who would be perfect for you. When you starve yourself, you actually send your metabolic process a message to slow down. It thinks it needs to conserve fuel and save energy in the form of calories, which helps insulate the body in the form of fat. Doesn't Mother Nature have an interesting sense of irony? This metabolic effect can make it harder to lose weight and leads to yo-yo dieting.

With the help of the dietitian, I began to learn how to substitute high-fat favorite foods with lower-fat ones and not feel as if I were missing out on anything. I also learned how to replace high-fat sour cream with yogurt and high-calorie sugar with substitutes or natural honey. Since I already had all the free stuff I had gotten in the doctor's office and the dietitian gave me even more *free* things, I was armed with the right information to make my dietary changes and not feel deprived when I ate.

Here are a few of my favorite substitutions:

- ✔ Use salsa for salad dressing. (Stick with mild or medium; hot overtakes a simple salad.)
- ✔ Use mustard instead of mayonnaise.
- ✔ Substitute cooking spray for oil or olive oil when oil is needed. (A combination of both can reduce fat even more, but still keep flavor.)
- ✔ Sauté instead of fry.
- ✔ Use low-fat yogurt in place of sour cream in baking recipes.
- ✔ Use frozen yogurt or tofutti instead of ice cream.
- ✔ Use honey for sugar if you want a natural substitute instead of an artificial one.
- ✔ Substitute soy or rice milk for milk or cream. (But watch the fat here too—there is nonfat soymilk, which is good if mixed with some vanilla soymilk for flavor.)
- ✔ Use veggie burgers instead of hamburgers.
- ✔ Substitute veggie cheese for real cheese. The real surprise is, you can hardly tell the difference!
- ✔ Drink diet soda, unsweetened iced tea, or water instead of high-calorie drinks and juices.
- ✔ Mix high-calorie juices with a bit of water.
- ✔ Substitute green tea for latte.
- ✔ Try California rolls or sushi with wasabi sauce and ginger instead of fried rice.

- ✔ Eat rice, couscous, or pasta instead of French fries. (A baked potato could do, if you can hold the butter and sour cream and eat it au naturel with maybe just salt and pepper—try that salsa again.)
- ✔ Mash cauliflower instead of potatoes.
- ✔ Substitute Egg Beaters/whites for whole eggs.
- ✔ Use cereals for snack foods (Coco Puffs can replace cookies), but watch the calories here too. I've seen cereal have anywhere between 90 to 220 calories per serving, and granolas in particular can be high in fat or sodium.
- ✔ Add wheat germ to salads, yogurt, and meals. The wheat germ will make you feel full on smaller portions and will add fiber, folic acid, and Vitamin E to your diet.
- ✔ Try a bagel instead of a muffin or Danish.
- ✔ Eat pretzels instead of potato chips.
- ✔ Mix olive oil with balsamic vinegar on bread instead of butter.
- ✔ Try hummus on bread instead of peanut butter.
- ✔ Use garlic with more garlic!

What are some of your own substitutes?

✔

✔

✔

✔

✔

✔

✔

✔

✔

Recipe Notations:

Always Be Prepared

Girl and Boy Scouts are taught to be prepared always. This was the rationale for making kids spend all day in the woods, rubbing two sticks together to make a fire, in case someone forgot to bring a Zippo on the camping trip. Sex education teachers teach that being prepared means always carrying a condom. I am going to add a new twist to these old standbys and apply it to food. I find that having healthy meals and snacks accessible helps me to make the right choices. If you know that you are always on the run, I would recommend that you:

- ✔ Buy precut salad fixing and vegetables. (Even carrots come already cut up.)
- ✔ Store frozen vegetables (not canned; they have too much added sodium as a preservative). You can prepare them quickly by steaming or microwaving them.
- ✔ Cook in bulk and freeze portion-size meals or use Healthy Choice or Lean Cuisine low-fat meals. Weight Watchers and Jenny Craig have frozen and other prepared products you can use without too much effort. But, be sure to check the sodium content on these items too.
- ✔ Carry your favorite healthy snacks with you to work or on a trip, so you are less tempted to buy an impulse snack.
- ✔ Keep pretzels in the cabinet for when you have a snack attack. They are the lowest-calorie alternative.

The Vitamin Debate

Do you need to take 47 different varieties of food supplements to be healthy? I don't really know for sure because there is a lot of debate on this subject, but I have made my decisions based on what I found to be the most credible evidence. Although I've heard some folks swear by shark cartilage and other supplements, I have read articles warning of the dangers of some of these food supplements because they are not Food and Drug Administration (FDA) controlled, so you don't really know how much of a substance is really in a pill, capsule, or tablet. Regardless, supplements have gotten to be more and more popular, and there is a lot of advertising promoting their use. However, be wary of anything that claims to cure 100 different and unrelated ailments—everything from hemorrhoids to tooth decay—and that will even help you lose weight. It is probably a good bet that it will not do much of anything.

However, according to the National Academy of Science, which created the *Recommended Dietary Allowance* (RDA) table, there are some basic vitamins your body does need, such as A, B (1, 2, 3, 6, 12), C, D, and E for development, immune system functioning, and metabolism. These vitamins can be found in a multivitamin, and that is the way I have chosen to go. Your diet should be giving you most of what you need, but a multivitamin should add what might have been missed. You also may need copper, zinc, and iron, which also can be found in a multivitamin. If you are on the Atkins or some other low-carb diet, a pill can replace the nutrients you are not getting in your food. If you feel you need extra calcium and magnesium or if your doctor has recommended it, then you would need an additional supplement. (This would apply more to menopausal women.) Overall, a multivitamin, such as Centrum with 100 percent of the Daily Value (DV) of all ingredients and a calcium/magnesium supplement is probably all you need. You can buy a multivitamin in the supermarket and not spend a lot of money.

Avoid any products that claim to be an "extra-special," "high-potency formula" "specially created" for this or that condition. There are no standards to back up any of these types of claims. There are also some vitamins you don't need "mega" amounts of because your body will not absorb them and you will just pee them away; considering how much some of these products cost, that is an unnecessary waste of your money. (Do you see the crude but true "pissing away your money" reference here?) Some products also claim to have added nutrients, which maybe true, but they may be in too small of an amount to make a difference or they may not be essential to your body's functioning.

The one thing you should look for is a **U.S. Pharmacopia (USP) seal** on the package that indicates that the ingredients are absorbable by humans. The package also must list an expiration date.

The most important thing to do with vitamins and food supplements is to discuss them with your primary care provider or dietitian to be sure that they are right for you. You may have an allergy to a substance in one of these products (some are made with shellfish for example) or experience negative side effects, or they may interact negatively with the prescription medication you are taking and weaken its effectiveness. Some of these products are also not kosher because of the additives or gells use in their production. So, don't forget to check if this is an issue for you as well.

I would avoid taking diet pills, diuretics, and/or laxatives as a means of losing weight. No evidence that I have seen recommends these drugs as a safe way to lose weight; they can be dangerous to your health. There are reports of athletes and other people who have died after using diet pills. If you don't believe me, ask your doctor.

Medication Notation

Food and vitamins do not replace prescription medication. You should ALWAYS take medication as prescribed, no matter how much better you are feeling or how well you think you have done with your diet, especially if you are taking medication for cholesterol, high blood pressure, or diabetes. Don't think you can beat the disease on your own. The mistake a lot of people make is to discontinue a medication prior to completing the prescription, which results in relapse or a worsening of the condition. If you are prescribed a medication to take everyday, take it everyday, not just when you feel bad. Consult with your primary care provider if you feel a medication is not working or if you are experiencing a negative side effect.

If your doctor gives you a prescription and you are not insured or can't afford the co-pay, discuss your financial situation with your doctor. Don't just skip the medication. You doctor may be able to prescribe a generic drug instead of the name brand; generic drugs have the same active ingredients as name-brand drugs, but cost less. Remember, medication can be discounted or free. Some drug companies have special programs that help patients purchase pharmaceuticals, especially if you are 65 years of age or older and are living on a fixed income. Find out who manufactures the drug you were prescribed and check their website for contact information. State programs may help with drug benefits, as can membership in various organizations.

It is important to remember that supplements, such as St. John's Wort, can interact with prescription medication. When you go to the doctor, be sure to tell him or her about all supplements and over-the-counter drugs that you take regularly.

Food Plans or Not

When I first began my quest towards a healthy diet, I considered joining a food plan. Basically, these are the structured meal plan programs that tell you which foods to eat and how much. Weight Watchers and Jenny Craig are probably the best known, but there is also the Atkins diet, which is a high-protein diet, the Perricone Prescription, LA Weight Loss, and the Zone diet. A more modified diet is the Slim Fast plan; it uses the shakes and bars that you can buy in any supermarket and is a lot cheaper than other types of plans, but it does not offer the personalized attention. I have talked to several people who had tried these plans and their success and failure rates varied. (This was not scientific research, mind you; just nosiness.) Those who have used the Atkins diet seem to be true believers, but they caution that Atkins is not for vegetarians since it is so protein based and that is where the beef is. I decided not to join any plan because I knew myself well enough to know that with my personality, lifestyle, and travel schedule, trying to follow a specific plan would not work best for me.

However, just because I am stubborn does not mean you should not check these options out for yourself. Some plans, like Weight Watchers and Jenny Craig, offer in-person peer support, assist with developing meal plans and food exchanges, and now even sell prepackaged prepared and frozen foods in most supermarkets. There are annual fees associated with joining these plans in addition to the cost of the food. The Atkins diet is based on a book written by the late Dr. Robert Atkins; you can follow this self-help guide on your own.

Many other diet doctors offer prescriptions and plans of their own. There are infomercials and advertisements touting different diet products and plans, but be wary of some of these. In deciding on a plan, you should consider membership and other fees, food costs, health risks, nutritional value, peer support, staff credentials, scientifically documented success rates (not just anecdotal reports of previously satisfied customers—get data), and yo-yo dieting effects (weight loss/gain over time). Ask a plan manger for all of that information, as well as about samples, cancellation fees, refunds, and trial memberships.

The key to success with any diet plan is its sustainability over the long run. As long as you are restricting calories and watching your portions, you will lose weight. So you can be successful with any of these diet plans in the short term. You need to make sure that any plan you decide to follow will be a lifestyle commitment you can make and that the foods you are eating are right for your body and the health risks you may have, such as diabetes or high cholesterol. Consult your primary care provider or a dietitian before making any radical changes to your diet.

Conduct Hydration, Ready Begin

In the Army, we used to jokingly refer to drinking water as "conducting hydration," because the military has a tendency to take the simplest of actions and make them complicated. We did most things as a unit, and the commander would yell out, "Ready, begin!" before we commenced most activities. When we took breaks (did I mention this was southern Texas in the summer?), there was one guy who would bark out, "Conduct hydration, ready begin." Isn't it the stupidest things that stick with you? But it is the one thought that comes to mind whenever I feel dehydrated.

Drinking water is important because our bodies are composed mostly of water and need water to survive. Ask your doctor if you must know the technical details, but I do know that lots of water helps me feel full and that is what I primarily care about. Although it has been debated on how much water the human body needs, *eight glasses of water a day (64 ounces)* seems to be what most of the experts say. However, remember that there is water in many foods that you eat and in juices, which counts too. If you drink caffeinated beverages, then you will need to drink more water, because caffeine acts like a diuretic. I do know that if I drink water at mealtimes, I feel full faster and don't eat as much, so that is a great side effect of conducting hydration.

And by the way, I have also read that tap water is just as good as bottled water. This means you don't need to spend a fortune on name brands you can't pronounce, unless you want to appear French and impress your friends and colleagues; then by all means *eau it up!*

Power Drinking

Gatorade, the ceremonial lime green beverage poured over coaches at the end of football games, actually is for drinking and is what is known as a sports drink (surprise!) or a power drink. Sports or power drinks have added electrolytes, carbohydrates, sodium, and potassium, which our bodies lose when we sweat. While you are exercising and really getting an intense cardio workout, sports drinks can be very helpful in keeping fluids moving to the muscles. Don't worry about the sugar that they contain; it is a low enough amount that you will burn it off. The sweetness will also entice you to drink more when you need it the most. Drink before working out and then after. If you're going on a long day of hiking or a bike trip, I'm told that it's good to drink every 20 minutes. I like Propel, which isn't as strong as Gatorade but is made by the same company.

The types of drinks you probably can do without are:

- ✔ **Caffeine drinks:** You don't need the jolt and will need to drink more water.
- ✔ **Protein drinks:** You don't need all of the calories unless you are really engaging in an intense or prolonged workout, like a four-day adventure race.
- ✔ **Colonics:** Doctors do not recommend that you cleanse your colon in this way, and if it is done incorrectly, it can be harmful.

Redecorate Your Plate

I once read an article that said most Americans have very little color in their meals. So, if you see a lot of brown and white when you look down at your dinner plate, it's time to redecorate your food with color. How simple is this advice? Go back to the food pyramid discussed under the *You Are What You Eat* tip. The real color is in the part of the pyramid, where all of the fruits and vegetables can be found. As part of your redecorating process, you need to follow the new pyramid. If you chart out your plate by dividing it into sections, make the meat or poultry serving smaller, ditch the mashed potatoes—use brown rice instead—and add a colorful veggie, which should take up half of the plate, and a salad. Orange (carrots, cantaloupes, yams) is a good color to add because orange fruits and vegetables are high in beta-carotene, an antioxidant, which helps lower cholesterol and prevents heart disease. The National Academy of Sciences suggests we need double the amount of beta-carotene than was originally thought. Vegetables that are a darker green have more of an antioxidant effect as well. Use cruciferous vegetables, such as broccoli, cauliflower, and cabbage, which are high in sulforaphane, a compound linked to reducing cancer risk. There are hundreds of different kinds of fruits and vegetables, so it should take you a long time to get bored. Have you ever had a pomegranate or a kumquat? Try new things. When you go shopping, make it a point to look for something you have never tasted before in the produce aisle and buy it. If you are not sure what to do with it, look it up online. I am sure you will find a delicious low-caloric recipe to try!

At breakfast, lunch, or for one of those snack times, add fruit. Get creative and go beyond a basic fruit salad. Experiment with mixing several kinds of fruit together with low-fat yogurt. Get a blender and mix different fruits with yogurt or soymilk, some ice, and a dash of vanilla or cinnamon. You can add Metamucil or wheat germ for the fiber. Experiment with some of your favorite fruits and make smoothies you can enjoy, especially as a cool-down treat in the summer. I also love adding cranberries to yogurt with low-fat granola. Remember to drink water, or try low-fat soymilk!

Spice It Up

When you cut fat, add flavor. Color will make the food look more appealing, which is important, but how the food actually tastes is what will keep you on the right nutritional track. It's not rocket science that we eat fatty foods because they taste good. Adding lots of broccoli to your plate and *no* butter might be hard to swallow (pun intended); get out that salsa or Japanese wasabi sauce, especially if you need the moisture in the consistency of the food that the butter used to provide your palate. Garlic with a little olive oil and a dash of vinegar is great over most veggies and will keep away vampires or anyone else you don't want to have bothering you.

In sandwiches, remember to hold the mayo but add mustard. There are so many kinds of mustards (deli, Chinese, Dijon, honey, etc.), you can experiment for years and not get bored. Can you say that about white goopy mayo? I think not! But wait! What about tuna fish or chicken salad? Yep, go ahead and make them with a bit of mustard too. You may want to water it down a bit, try it with yogurt, or go a different route with the tuna and add lemon with salt and pepper (or any other spices you may like). If you think you can handle the "add fruit" tip, go ahead and slice in pineapple bits or mandarin oranges.

Salads can be spiced up in many ways too. Be unconventional when tossing the high-fat dressings. Salsa and wasabi sauce are my favorite additions to a salad, but try other spices or toss in fruit or nuts to give a simple house salad a bit more flair.

Instead of traditional sour cream dips, use guacamole (avocados are high in fat, but it is the good kind), hummus, or baba ganosh (eggplant spread) for your vegetable platters.

Cold cuts or deli meats can be very high in fat, sugar, and sodium depending upon how they are processed, so avoid them like the plague, and look for veggie sandwiches or at least lean turkey breast (not turkey roll). Add a bit of unprocessed cheese or soy cheese for the calcium, and as a treat. Cover with sprouts and use whole-grain bread (not white bread). While at the deli counter also watch the salads that are prepared with a great deal of mayonnaise. You are better off buying the packages of shredded slaw in the supermarket produce section and making your own, so you can control the amount of mayo, if any at all.

Oh, and remember to hold the salt. This is the one spice to ax. Salt and sodium can lead to high blood pressure and make you retain water and feel and look bloated. Who wants that? Make sure to use garlic powder, not garlic salt. Watch out for blended spices; they usually have a lot of salt in them too. Try adding curry powder, pepper, or blackening seasoning instead. Experiment with dill, cilantro, sage, rosemary, basil, coriander, or any other herbs that add zest and flavor. The fresher the herbs, the better they will taste and the more flavor the food will have.

Eat Like a Cow

This is my favorite tip. It is actually good to eat like a cow because cows graze in the fields, eating a little bit here and a little bit there. Of course, they look like cows, but that's because they don't actually get enough exercise to be able to jump over a log, much less the moon. Don't worry that you are going to overeat. Keep in mind that it is better to *eat six times a day* than to overdo it two or three times a day. A wonderful friend from my Guacamole Club is a beanpole. We call her the "grazer" because she is always snacking on something. She takes a few bites here and there and then moves on to do something else. This is the way we should all eat—oh, and by the way, she considers chocolate and licorice essential food groups, but manages to stay slim because she controls her portion sizes and nibbles here and there, which keeps her metabolism charged.

Medical evidence suggests that grazing is a healthy approach to eating because there is a hormone, called ghrelin, that stimulates our appetites when our stomachs are empty and makes us feel even hungrier. The best way to keep ghrelin levels down is to give the stomach what it wants—food. By eating six smaller meals per day, you are lowering the hormone level that tells your brain that your body needs fuel. When you skip meals or try to deprive yourself too much, ghrelin kicks in and sends the brain signals that your fuel level is too low. It's like when the "check gas gauge" light in your car goes on (no doubt in the middle of the night while traveling lost and alone on the highway). When this happens, you develop cravings and overeat later. This has led many of us down the path of yo-yo dieting that results in our weight fluctuations. Therefore, if you eat and then snack every three hours, like the "grazer," you keep your hormones in check and your appetite under control.

To be a grazer, keep healthy snacks in the kitchen or at your desk, so that you can munch a few pretzels or reenergize with fruit. Bananas or a container of low-fat yogurt can save the day. The most common mistake people make is to skip breakfast. When you do that, you have a tendency to eat more, later because you are out of fuel. So always make sure to take a banana, orange, apple, or grapes with you to start your day right. (Take along a napkin and a baggie to keep your snack spot clean.)

Also, grazing will help you feel more energized during the day and more mentally alert. You will feel as if you can get more accomplished and will even have the energy for a late-in-the-day workout. You won't feel deprived and will feel better about what you are trying to accomplish with your new approach to a healthy lifestyle.

Whoa It Down

When it comes to eating, I have superhuman powers. I can finish dinner in a single bound. I am usually almost done by the time my husband has gotten comfortable, poured a drink, and salted his food. He is usually still chewing while I am doing the dishes. Mystified by his ability to walk away from a half-full plate, I ask him repeatedly if he is *sure* he *really* liked the meatloaf since he didn't finish it all. He reassures me about my culinary skills, but rushes out of the room (perhaps in an attempt to avoid the dishes). Regardless, in my household this phenomenon is indicative of two things: the childhood attitude that I have from having grown up to "clean my plate" and the science of metabolism and digestion.

Leaving my mother out of this, and focusing instead on the metabolic process involved, the scientific answer to this mysterious behavior is that, by eating more slowly, my husband is actually allowing his stomach the time it needs to send signals to his brain, alerting it that his stomach is full. It takes about 10 minutes for the sensation of being full to set in, so the slower we eat, the quicker our brain catches on. Thus, we don't overeat. If you don't rush through your meals, you will enjoy your food more and feel less deprived because your brain will feel satiated too. At my house, I've had to make a conscientious effort to eat slower, and my husband has more of an opportunity to help with the dishes.

The Supermarket Zone—Buyer Beware

✔ **Read the labels.** This is the dangerous part. *If it doesn't make it into the shopping cart at the store, it won't be in your home to tempt you to eat it.* Obvious, huh? So, why not just keep it out? This is not always that easy. Sure, you know to avoid certain high-fat, high-calorie foods, but what about all the new products that seem to come in the green boxes, which make low-fat, low-calorie, or low-carb claims to be better for your health? Well, it all comes down to reading the labels, which, if you have gotten all the right free stuff from your doctor's office or dietitian, you should be an expert at by now. The part of the label I pay the most attention to is the cholesterol and fat information. But if you are a diabetic or are carbohydrate sensitive, you may need to pay more attention to the number of total and net carbohydrates. The experts tell me that a regular 2,000-calorie a day diet should contain 25 to 30 percent fat. Since my cholesterol is high, I aim for 1,800 calories and no more than 15 percent fat. Products that are 5 to 7 percent fat don't even make it to the checkout counter. Learn how to read those side panels. Usually what less fat means is that the green box version is less or has half of the fat calories than the regular product of the same brand. Half of a *gazillion* calories, though, is still too many. In addition, the fat may have been taken out, but salt, flour, and/or sugar may have been added (manufacturers know about the less fat/more spice rule too), so the overall calorie contents may be the same or even more than the regular brand. (Shame on them!) Additionally, if the sodium content has gone up, the food is not a good choice for you or could even be worse than the original if you have high blood pressure. Be an educated consumer and don't buy new products until you have had a chance to research them.

- ✔ **Another word of caution:** Just because the low-fat version has half the calories, you can't have twice as many of them. Read what the portion sizes are. Take the suggested amount out of the box, put the box away, and then enjoy it slowly! Total self-denial would be very self-defeating, so switch to the lower-in-calorie snacks, but just be aware of the side panel contents and how much of it you use.

- ✔ **It costs more to shop healthy.** Yup. I'm not going to try to lie to you about that, especially if you want to try the more exotic or organic fruits and vegetables. But to save money, you can buy fruits and vegetables that are in season or are on sale. Buy more and freeze them when they are cheaper. Don't buy the precut veggies and salads, unless you are more concerned about saving time than money. If price and not practicality is the issue, then save the money and cut them up yourself and store them in portion sizes. I also buy the store brand on the packaged items to save the money. And of course there are always coupons! You may also want to buy the larger size of an item, such as olive oil, because you may be getting twice as much but not for twice the price. Look at it this way: tofu doesn't cost as much as sirloin, so you can save money by cutting out the high-calorie items too.

- ✔ **Perimeter shop.** Stick to the outer edges of the supermarket and avoid the aisles, except for toilet paper. The perimeter of the supermarket has all of the fresh produce, the dairy counter, the meats and seafood, and the bakery, where you can get whole-grain bread (be sure to stay away from the cupcakes). The aisles are filled with all of the processed and canned foods that are higher in the calories, fats, carbohydrates, and sodium that you don't need anyway.

- ✔ **Do not go to the supermarket hungry.** When you're hungry, you have more of a tendency to overbuy things you should not have or things you really don't need. You may also be more susceptible to those last-minute temptation items at the checkout counter. Supermarket owners are counting on you making that impulse buy, which is what they put those items by the registers. Eat before you go to the supermarket, or at least drink lots of water first so you need to hurry home to pee.

When Only Chocolate Will Do

When it absolutely, positively, undoubtedly, has to be chocolate, then go for it. We all have those days when we just have to have it, can't live without it, and would give up sex for a Hershey's Kiss. But there are some rules to follow here too that can leave you feeling less guilty after you indulge.

First, stick with dark chocolate; it doesn't have the same amount of fat calories as milk chocolate (because of the added milk) and white chocolate, which is very high in fat. Dark chocolate is made mostly from the cacao plant, so it does contain flavonoids, other minerals, and antioxidants, which are good for lowering cholesterol and reducing heart disease. Avoid macadamia or other high-fat nut additives or other extra goo that only adds calories and detracts from the chocolate you are craving. Portion control is important here too. Don't reach for the super size Kit-Kat bar, but rather take a serving (look at the bag label) of bite-size chocolates. I recommend sticking with Dove or Hershey's Kisses dark chocolates and have one or two. Don't just sit down with an entire mud pie. Take a small piece, sit down comfortably, eat slowly, and enjoy it. Wash it down with a diet soda or water to get the sweetness off your taste buds. If you rush or don't savor your treat, it won't seem like you have had it at all and the craving is less likely to go away. You will also feel more rewarded it you take the time to indulge yourself completely. So go ahead and celebrate your 40th birthday, a successful client presentation, or back-to-school day. You deserve it.

What if you've just gotta have *real* cheesecake? Share it with a group. You're less likely to scarf up the whole thing in front of everybody. Have a few bites and proclaim victory!

Go Nuts, But Not Crazy

Whether to eat nuts or not has made me crazy! They are a great source of protein, vitamins, and antioxidants, and some are known to lower cholesterol. They are also a great source of magnesium, which helps fight heart arrhythmia, blocked arteries, diabetes, osteoporosis, and high blood pressure. More magnesium in your diet can also reduce pain associated with fibromyalgia, migraines, and muscle cramps. However, nuts are high in fat and calories. I checked the jar of peanut butter I have in my cabinet; it has 200 calories and 140 fat calories for a two-tablespoon serving. That is spreading it on real thin, I'd say. But most articles I have read recommend eating nuts as part of a healthy diet. So, what is the real deal?

There are three secrets to eating nuts.

1. Make sure to stick with the ones that have fewer fat calories, such as almonds, walnuts, pecans, and peanuts. You can also try soy nuts or seeds, such as pumpkin and sunflower, which are even higher in magnesium. Avoid the higher-fat nuts: macadamia, cashew, and Brazil.

2. Use nuts sparingly. A serving is 1 ounce, which should fit in the palm of your hand.

3. Mix nuts with cereals and dried fruit as a snack or chop them up and serve them over salads or vegetables.

Restaurant Fare

I love to eat out. Restaurants are one of my favorite social experiences. I enjoy trying new foods. The ambiance and variations in presentation are an important part of the meal for me as well. But I am also keenly aware that restaurants want you to keep coming back. To do that, they often overload patrons with food and spare no expense on the fat. How to maintain my dining-out lifestyle and not add hidden fat and calories to my day was a question I faced. There were tricks to be learned here too.

On the menu:

- ✔ Check the salad selections. Some restaurants have gotten very creative with what they will put over lettuce to make it exotic and tempting.
- ✔ Ask for salsa (if that will do) or low-fat salad dressing (which most restaurants now have). If all else fails, go with a honey mustard; it is lower in fat than other regular dressings. Of course, get all dressings on the side so you can control how much goes on the salad.
- ✔ Not in the mood for another salad? Check the fish. There are scientific reasons why fish is good for you: it is loaded with omega-3, which can even help fight high cholesterol and is good for your bones (not so good if you swallow a fish bone, so get it filleted). Order it sautéed in olive oil, if possible, or baked, never fried. Watch the shellfish because it is higher in cholesterol and may not be the best choice. In a Chinese restaurant, shrimp and tofu are actually great palate pleasers, believe it or not. Try it for yourself, but over brown or white rice, not fried.
- ✔ Since everything tastes like chicken anyway, why not just go with it? It should be without the skin and not fried. Stay away from the Colonel.
- ✔ Anything in an Alfredo or a cream sauce was probably invented by the Mafia because it is meant to kill you. Don't even go there. A plain marinara (no meat) can be great over vegetables and pasta.
- ✔ If you're like me and you must have the bread, especially when it comes to the table steaming, go for it, but skip the butter. If you are a true bread lover, it's really all about the bread anyway.
- ✔ Don't super size or get appetizers. In most restaurants the portions are enough to fill you up anyway. I read recently how restaurant food servings in America have almost doubled in the

last 30 years. A muffin has become a deadly weapon in some states, so beware!

- ✔ Don't clean your plate, no matter how much this used to make your mother happy. In spite of what she may have told you, leftover food won't send her to an early grave. Section off food (not the veggies, but the carbs) on your plate to the side even before you begin to eat and don't eat what you have sectioned off. It is a lot easier to measure the extra food while it is all right in front of you. Get the waiter to wrap it up as soon as he can so it does not tempt you; have it for lunch the next day. Drink lots of water and be inspired by your willpower to not finish the whole meal.

- ✔ Eat slowly. When we eat too fast, we are not paying attention to the sensation of feeling full that we get. The more slowly and more relaxed you eat, the fuller you will feel and the easier it will be to not clean your plate. After all, isn't relaxation part of the reason to eat out? (This advice goes for when you're at home too and no one is watching you shovel in leftover lasagna.)

- ✔ Remember the movie *When Harry Met Sally*? When ordering, Sally asked the waiter tons of questions and gave him all kinds of special instructions. Harry thought she was adorable, and the waiter brought her just what she wanted. Well, don't be afraid to be a Sally in a restaurant. Don't be embarrassed to ask about how food is prepared and make your dietary requirements known. If you are dining with the right people, they will think you are adorable too (if not see the section on *Positive People*) and leave the waiter a little extra in the tip for his trouble. He will forgive you for taking up his time, and besides, you probably won't be seeing him again any time soon anyway.

- ✔ Do keep track of the restaurants and takeout places that meet your needs and stick with those as your regular dining spots. They will be more likely to accommodate you, especially if the waiter knows you are a good tipper. Restaurants that are your regular haunts will be happy to accommodate you and the friends you bring in to dine with you.

Holiday Feasts and Celebrations

Uh-oh! Aunt Evelyn's surprise party invitation has come in the mail or the office annual holiday party will be catered. Now what? Should you feign fever and skip the festivities, or just go and blow your entire month of dieting at one gala? Neither one: girls just want to have fun, right? Here's how to do it and have a great guilt-free time and no regrets the next morning. (Well, not including any rendezvous in the copy room with the hottie from marketing.)

Here's what I do to make it a night to remember:

- ✔ **Dress the part.** If you are wearing form-fitting, sexy clothes, you won't feel as tempted by the plum pudding. The tight waistband will remind you that you really are full and you don't need one more sugar cookie. If you don't feel like a fat schlub, you won't act like one. Besides, everyone will be telling you how great you look so you won't have time to eat anyway.
- ✔ **Eat before you go.** This may sound dumb when all of that food is awaiting you, but that is the point. If you starve yourself before a night out and are ready to eat a horse when you get there, you most likely will. If you are already full on your regular healthy foods, then you won't be as interested in the fatty smorgasbord awaiting you and it will be easier to walk away.
- ✔ **Use the same rules as when eating in restaurants.** Believe it or not, I have been able to find salads, vegetables, and fruit at parties. Reach for extra yams (without the cute little marshmallows), and just have a small slice of the ham.
- ✔ **Bring your own dish.** Most hostesses won't be offended if you show up with your favorite low-calorie recipe. (You just may not want to tell them that the cheese is really a tofu substitute.) Call your hostess in advance and tell her you have a favorite dish you would like to share with her guests and ask if it would be OK to

bring it along. Then serve yourself from it first and taste whatever else might be on your list of fat-free foods.

- ✔ **Take a taste.** We all know you are going to eat chocolate again so have one small piece of the homemade fudge. Carefully pick the dessert or cream sauce, which everyone is raving about, and have a bite. Enjoy it slowly and then wash it down with water or a diet soda. (I find this helps to get the sweet sensation out of my mouth so I don't yearn for more.) The diet soda (or anything fizzy) advantage is that the bubbles will add to your sense of feeling full too.

- ✔ **Watch the alcohol.** You know what happens when you drink too much: you lose your willpower to say no to things that are bad for you. (That is how you ended up in the backseat of what-was-his-name-again's GTO after your high school prom.) Alcohol is also loaded with calories so remember to count them too. Know that drinking excess alcohol over the long term increases abdominal fat (the proverbial beer belly) and your risk for heart disease and type-2 diabetes. Moderate drinking is considered no more than two drinks a week for a man and one for a woman. (Keep that in mind too when you are driving.) Drinking should not be everyday. When you are drinking, stay away from the food table, so you won't nibble subconsciously.

- ✔ **Share the gift basket.** Someone who meant well has left you a box of Godiva on your desk for your birthday. Take the one or two pieces that you covet and then take the box out to the typing pool and share the wealth. You will spare yourself the guilt of knowing you've hidden it in your bottom drawer and will add to your popularity in the office, which can come in handy the next time you need 50 copies collated and stapled in an hour.

What if you did overdo it during the holidays or on vacation? Even if you gained a few pounds, if you have followed some of the other tips and have increased your metabolic rate, you can probably lose them within two or three days after getting back to your normal routine.

On the Road Again

Your boss has decided to send you to Duluth to represent your company at the 27th Annual Sprocket Salesperson Convention. You know you will be working long hours, attending business lunches and evening receptions. All of your meals for the next week will be in restaurants.

It's vacation time! You are off on a long-awaited cruise to the Keys with the man of your dreams whom you met at the sprocket convention last fall. It couldn't be more perfect. There is nothing to do but soak up the sun and down some piña coladas. What's the problem?

For most of us, dieting and exercising are part of our daily routine. When we change that routine, we change our habits. Vacation or any travel is often viewed as "time off" from our daily schedule, so we tend to use it as an excuse to eat more than we should. We order fried shrimp instead of broiled and we even go for the key lime pie (especially if we are already in the Keys) when we otherwise would resist. So, what to do when traveling?

- ✔ **Review the tips on restaurant fare.** Eating out is eating out whether you are in town or out. When you check into a hotel, ask at the desk for low-fat or vegetarian dining recommendations.

- ✔ **Don't book trips where meals are included.** Look for plans that give you the option of skipping meals. You can get more sightseeing time this way and burn calories while climbing castle stairs. You should be able to find cheaper food places (as long as they look clean and safe) along the way. I have found pizza in most cities in the 22 countries I have visited, and it's always cheap too, which leaves me more money for shopping.

- ✔ **Find the time on the road for a workout.** Most hotels, even the smaller ones, have exercise rooms with some equipment. If not, they usually have some arrangement with a local fitness center. If you have joined a gym that is part of a franchise, check their travel policy before you go. Most fitness chains have locations around the world, and you can use facilities as a guest member. For example, Curves, with over 8,000 franchises worldwide, allows its members the option of getting travel passes when they will be away from their home club. Ask at the hotel desk when you check in about fitness options. There might even be an indoor pool! Instead of plopping down on the bed between the convention exhibit show and the reception, take 15 minutes or half an hour and get on the treadmill or stationary bike or go to the pool. Resorts are usually beautiful, so get on the sneakers and go for a brisk walk. There is no better place to walk than on a sandy beach. Sand provides added resistance and enhances your workout, plus the view is great to clear your mind and refresh your spirit. Oh, and beach? Swim!

- ✔ **Plan an active/healthy vacation.** This could be the opportunity to do the whitewater rafting, skiing, or hiking that you have always dreamed of. Challenge yourself and look for activities that will cater to your skill level. Most resorts, ranches, and vacation coordinators are prepared to handle beginners, intermediate, and advanced participants, and can book you accordingly. Many of these types of vacations offer wholesome meals as well, so you don't have to worry about the food.
- ✔ **Take a spa day.** Find the time for a massage, facial, and/or salon visit. It will keep you in touch with your goals for healthy living and will provide you with a real treat. Isn't that why you went on vacation in the first place?
- ✔ **Pack a snack.** Take along some of your favorite low-cal treats when you head out on the road. You can skip the bacon and egg breakfast by having a low-fat granola bar in your bag, and then just pick up juice or coffee and a fruit.
- ✔ **Frequent terminal miles.** When you've arrived at the airport two hours early and it only took 20 minutes to check your bags and clear security, walk the terminals instead of hitting the (overpriced) snack bar or sitting aimlessly at the gate. I've easily walked for half an hour while changing planes at O'Hare International awaiting the next leg of my flight. Dodging hurried

passengers and beeping carts makes for a great cardio workout! Just don't miss your flight.

Put a Hold on Your Hunger

Controlling appetite is key to controlling weight gain. *Duh!* If it were only that simple, though, right? But think back to a time when you were really busy and even though you felt like a cougar was pacing around in your stomach, you didn't have time to take a break. Then an hour later, when you were finished and could take a break, the hunger pains had gone away. Well, maybe I am just easily distracted, but I know that when I am engrossed in a book or trapped in a car and cannot eat right away, the sensations that make me feel hungry do fade. I think I got through my high school first-period chemistry class that way (as a big breakfast skipper back then). However, I did not exactly ace high school chemistry, so skipping breakfast was probably not such a good idea, and it still isn't. When you are trying to lose weight, don't skip meals, especially breakfast. Skipping meals will only lead to binge eating later in the day when your body craves the quick-fix energy that usually comes from sugar. (Read the *Eat like a Cow* tip.)

There are other things you can do to control hunger:

- ✔ Drink water or diet soda or anything with bubbles to help fill you up. Keep a full glass on your desk and sip away.
- ✔ Take a quick walk or do a short cardio workout. When your energy is in your muscles, it's not in your stomach.
- ✔ Keep your mind and hands busy, so you won't eat when you are bored. Start a hobby, do a crossword puzzle or knit, especially when watching TV, so you are not tempted to head to the kitchen during commercial breaks.
- ✔ Make healthy snacks easily accessible.
- ✔ Brush your teeth or use mouthwash to keep you from feeling like you want to eat.

- ✔ Use sugar-free gum or mints to keep your mouth feeling fresh when you are out and about.
- ✔ Call a friend or your diet pal for emotional support.
- ✔ Consult with your primary care provider before taking any appetite suppressants (if you feel you must take them).

EXERCISE TIPS

Now, here is the part that might be the hardest to hear. To really lose weight and live a healthier lifestyle, you have to get off of the couch. But remember, in this book, you can count shopping as exercise. Studies have shown that if you exercise for at least 30 minutes three times a week, you can improve your health. This becomes even more important when you reach the ripe old age of 30, when cardiovascular endurance and muscle strength begin to decrease. American Heart Association research shows that 10 minutes of exercise three times a day is good for your heart's health. You should be able to find an hour of time during your week to get your heart rate up, especially if you are like me and being 30 years old was the good old days. Just get moving! Exercise is the best anti-aging medicine around.

Besides weight loss, exercise is actually good for you for other reasons too. Exercise can help reduce stress and tension after a day with your kids or when your boss is on a tear. It does stimulate your brain and helps keep your mind sharper. It improves your muscle tone and physical strength while controlling your appetite, so you will look better without even having to think about dieting. Exercise improves flexibility, so you can really impress your friends with how well you can reach behind yourself to catch a fleeing child from the curb. Other health advantages to working out include getting a better night's sleep and reducing the dark circles under your eyes, mood elevation, lowering your blood pressure, increasing your immunity, controlling your cholesterol, and reducing your diabetes risk. And just think about how much better you will feel about yourself and what you have accomplished.

There are three primary types of exercise that you can do: *cardio (vascular) or aerobics*, *strength*, and *flexibility* exercises. With a cardio workout, you are increasing your heart rate and burning the most fat. Strength training involves lifting weights or using resistance to tone muscles. Flexibility exercise, such as yoga, stretches muscles and improves breathing.

Take time to develop your own Fitness Plan on the following page and log your activities on a calendar so you can monitor your progress. Think about all the possible things you could do that would increase your activity level. What would you like to add to your own Fitness Plan?

FITNESS PLAN			
Activity:	**Day**	**Time:**	**Place:**
Example: Skating Walk to lunch	Saturdays Mon–Fri	1:00 pm noon	state park near office

Having trouble coming up with ideas? Don't worry. The next few pages should help you take care of that. Pick out some tips that you like and log them into your Fitness Plan. Make sure you record them in your daily planner or Palm Pilot, so you don't forget to do them or won't give away that time slot.

Set a Workout Schedule

Set a specific workout time and add it to your schedule; otherwise the day will go by and you'll feel too tired or think that it has gotten too late to exercise. Just as you make appointments with everyone and for everything else that is important in your day, do the same thing for yourself with physical activity. Block out a half hour in your daily planner that works for you and make that your time. Be careful not to give that time away to other things that might come up. People are very understanding if you ask to meet them an hour later or earlier.

I started my workout with my stationary bike. After I dusted it off, I got on it every day at 6:00 in the evening. It was the first thing I did when I got home from work. I began with 15-minute rides, which was all I could take at the time, and then worked my way up to an hour. I have continued to do this regularly for over three years now. When I began working from my home as a consultant, I discovered that I had to keep to the same schedule and not give away my fitness time; otherwise I would lose my routine. This is an important point to consider if you are not employed outside of your home, but still have lots of people and animals who place demands on your time. Set a schedule for yourself first and don't give away your time unless it is urgent.

Think about whether it would be best for you to exercise in the morning, afternoon, evening, or at night. Pick an exact time and keep that hour. People really will understand that this is your schedule. Set a good pace for yourself so that you are still getting your heart rate up, but will have the endurance to last the entire session.

Can't keep to your schedule or you are running late? It's better to fit in 20 minutes than skip your workout altogether because you missed your hour. Try to plan for lateness by keeping your sneakers and workout clothes handy. If you constantly have to rework your schedule, maybe you should reevaluate your fitness plan and change the time of day you have scheduled your workout. If you do have to miss a workout session, make sure to fit it in the next day to fit it in, even if it is an abbreviated session. Get in a "quickie" just to keep your routine going. I have often heard people say that they missed their workout a few times and just got out of the habit and quit altogether.

Make Working Out Enjoyable

Your workout should be your playtime. When we where children, we would yell out to our moms, "*I am going out to play*!" Then we would run, jump rope, hula-hoop, ride bikes, and climb. As adults, we refer to those same activities as "exercise" or "workouts." How did these activities go from being fun to sounding like tasks? We need to mentally and emotionally reclaim our childhood enthusiasm for fun and games and approach physical activity as if it were our school recess time again, not just another item on our to-do list. This is your time for you, so indulge in it. Turn loose your inner child and have a blast! At the Curves where I have done fitness training, I loved to hand a hula-hoop to a 50-something woman and watch her gleefully toss it over her head and gyrate as it hit her hips! Find ways to make your exercise time fun.

For example, I couldn't think of anything more boring than sitting on a stationary bike and pedaling to nowhere. A minute felt like an hour, not because I was exhausted, but because I was bored. So, I added books, magazines, crossword puzzles, the telephone (although I found it helpful to tell callers about the source of my heavy breathing and ask if they didn't mind talking to me while I was on my bike), and the ultimate distraction: TV. Amazingly, I could easily pedal faster longer as my old favorite companion entered the arena. It was the dawn of a new day for the couch potato! Initially, I had an old 13-inch portable TV in the bedroom when I first started my workout routine. When my husband saw just how dedicated I was becoming, he supported the practice by surprising me with a 25-inch TV with cable and a remote control one day when I came home from work. There was no turning back! I had to keep going.

Armed with a remote control, I soon made a full hour on the bike. (Thank goodness for *X-File* reruns, which kept me so distracted while on the edge of my seat, I easily pedaled 12 miles!)

However, it is important to concentrate on the workout and make sure you haven't slacked off while reading *You Can Too.* (Who else's book would I plug here?) I have to admit that fitness gurus argue against engaging in other activities while you are working out; they feel you should concentrate on your workout to keep up the intensity. To that I say, "Are they kidding?" If I had to concentrate on every step I took while jogging, I wouldn't make it to the lamppost on the corner. I need the music or the TV to help me feel comforted and soothed while working out, which also makes me feel I made the most of my time for me. It feels great to know I burned 500 calories on my stationary bike while reading the latest Government Accounting Office Report.

I added other activities to my routine and tried tennis, swimming, hiking, circuit training, kickboxing, and yoga. My Guacamole Club friends who indulged in many of these outings can tell great stories of all the mishaps and missteps, but the key was the sweating that happened. The laughs are an added bonus. I have also used a headset and have listened to music and lecture tapes when I am out jogging on my own and have no one to talk to as a distraction. The music actually helps me feel like moving, which is good since most people use music for dancing.

And let's not leave out dancing. Can you make exercise any more fun? Get back out there with your friends and shake your booty. You can try all kinds of dance classes, everything from belly dancing to Zydeco. You can swing, tap, samba, mambo, hip hop, and, if you must, disco. Check with your local community recreational center for classes.

After about a year and a half of exercising behind closed doors on my bedroom bike and 40 pounds lighter, I actually got up the nerve to join a fitness center, which has added to my choice of activities. (See *To Gym or Not to Gym* tip.) I can go to yoga, aerobics, body-sculpting, Pilates, kickboxing, or step classes. At Curves, there is circuit training. There is also plenty of equipment and trainers who can teach you how to use the equipment properly, so you don't turn yourself in to a very sore pretzel.

Using a variety of equipment is important. Not only will it keep you from getting bored and quitting, but *cross training* will also reduce your risk for overuse or injury to one set of muscle groups. If you have played tennis one day, you may want to go to a Pilates class the next and lift weights the day after that. In this way, you are balancing out your activities by cross training from a cardio to flexibility to a strength routine.

Believe it or not, you will actually become addicted to your exercise time—or should I say your playtime? —And you will crave it when you miss it. The adrenaline and the endorphins your body will be producing will make you feel mentally and physically more relaxed, yet energized after each session. You will discover that you will begin to look forward to this time and enjoy the sense of accomplishment when you are done.

But don't forget to take a day off and rest your body. If you become obsessive about your workout schedule, you can cause muscle damage and fatigue. Injuries will cause you to go longer periods without exercising at all, and that puts you at risk for quitting altogether. Since you will achieve results from 30 minutes, three days a week, you won't need to do aerobics everyday.

Walk Before You Run

Take this rule literally. Walking is the easiest way to start an exercise routine since you don't have to learn anything or go anywhere special. The U.S. Surgeon General recommends that 30 minutes every day of moderate activity, such as walking, can improve your overall health. Start with 10 minutes three days a week. Then go to 15 minutes, and then 30 minutes. After lunch or dinner, walk it off. I remember doing this with my mom and sister as a kid. Mom used to like to walk around the block after dinner (and look in all the neighbors' windows to see how they decorated their houses; boy would we laugh, mostly at her).

Get adventurous and pick a day and find a nice trail to hike! There are wonderful national, state, and regional parks nestled into neighborhoods all across America. Find out more about your local community or state park by looking in your phone book under *Recreation and Parks*. Get on their mailing lists so that you can find out more about the activities they offer throughout the year. The other good news is that most of these parks are free. My husband and I had lived in the same area in Silver Spring, Maryland, for years before we ever went to a fantastic arboretum just a few miles from our home. It had paths through exotic gardens and every type of flora and fauna imaginable. There was even a pond loaded with frogs to watch. Another regional park has a small lake where we were able to rent rowboats or paddleboats at very reasonable rates. We have had some real romantic afternoons rowing around (mostly in circles) on the lake, eating sandwiches, and feeding the geese. I have hiked trails there too and have enjoyed watching deer run through the woods.

If biking is more your thing, most of these parks have trails to accommodate bikes, and I have seen families riding together on all types of bikes.

Short Walks and Quick Fixes

Don't have that much time during your busy day to go walking? Walk during your lunch hour. Walk to the restaurant or take-out place, and then walk when you go to your bank or to run other errands. Or just walk. Leave sneakers under your desk or in a locker and put them on for 15 minutes and walk around the building where you work. It might not be the most exciting trip, but it at least gets your blood pumping. The President's Council on Physical Fitness suggests getting in 10,000 steps daily. You can measure your steps by wearing a pedometer, and track how much walking you do every day.

Not even enough time for a walk? Close your office door and do jumping jacks or jump rope (or pretend to) for as long as you can. Do a quick repetition of push-ups (up against the wall is OK) and/or crunches. Take a 10-minute trip up and down the stairs while you wait for a fax to go through.

No time to shower after working up a sweat? Lots of busy people who stay fit keep baby wipes with their workout clothes and some body mist and deodorant. Wipe, spray, roll, and apply a little fresh makeup, and you can be good to go for the rest of your day!

Increase Your Cardio

Ready to increase your workout? You have done your 10 minutes, 15 minutes, and 30 minutes of walking and are feeling pumped. You have started to consider yourself an urban athlete. Now you're ready to take on the next level and want to do more of a cardio workout, which is good because aerobic or cardio workouts strengthen your heart and lungs. In order to get more out of your workout routine, you need to increase your level of activity so that it also increases your heart rate. In a moment of weakness one spring, I signed up for the Army 10-miler in the fall (someone had to finish last) and spent the summer training for it. I don't know if I will ever do it again, but it was a good way to get me motivated and challenge myself to increase my cardio routine.

However, remember to warm up first for about 10 to 15 minutes before aerobics.

You can increase your cardio by:

- ✔ Power walking, jogging, or running outdoors or on a treadmill
- ✔ Biking on a trail or on a stationary bike with a higher set resistance
- ✔ Steady swimming
- ✔ Enrolling in a step class or using a step machine
- ✔ Jumping rope for as long as you can take it
- ✔ Doing aerobics, spinning, kickboxing, or belly-dancing classes

If you are really working hard enough, *your* target heart rate *will increase to between 60 to 80 percent of your maximum heart rate; 70 percent is ideal.* You can calculate your maximum heart rate by subtracting your age from 220. So, if you are 40 years old, your *maximum* heart rate for one minute is 180, but you will start to burn fat calories when your heart rate is over 120. You can check your heart rate by taking your pulse after about 10 minutes of cardio and then compare it to the 10-second heart rate for your age group from the chart on the following page. Multiply your 10-second heart rate to see what it would be for the full minute (if you are that interested in doing the extra math).

TARGET HEART RATE

Age	10-second heart rate
20	20-27
25	20-26
30	19-25
35	19-25
40	18-24
45	18-23
50	17-23
55	17-23
60	16-22
65	16-21
70	15-20

You can use this chart to determine your target heart rate. If you are above your target heart rate or find it difficult to talk or feel dizzy or queasy, you should slow down. You may be on your way to looking great, but think about how silly you would look with a grass stain on your forehead from passing out on the track.

Flexibility Training—Start Your Day with a Stretch

Give yourself 10 to 15 minutes every morning to stretch out your body and meet your need to get in a *flexibility training session*. This will release endorphins and give you extra pep in your step to help start your day.

After you've rolled out of bed, do a series of toe touches (don't lock your knees), arm stretches, neck and shoulder rolls, sit-ups, push-ups, leg lifts, and squats. Yoga poses are all about flexibility, so learning a few of those can be very helpful in meeting this goal. (See *Hatha, Anusara, Sivananda, and Pilates* tip in the Stress Management section for more information on yoga.) Stretches work best and improve flexibility if done in slow steady motions. Reach as far as you can and hold for a count of 10. Breathe into the stretch. Do about three or four repetitions of 10. Then relax, switch sides, or move onto the next pose. Start slowly, though, and work your way up by adding stretches and repetitions. Don't increase the intensity of your workout too much too soon. The basic rule I've heard is to add only about 10 percent to your routine each week. (See *Warm Muscles Are Happy Muscles* tip for more detailed stretching instructions.)

You can add a *balance ball* to make it more interesting. Balance balls (sometimes called exercise or therapy balls) should reach about mid-thigh when inflated and come with instructions on the different exercises you can do to improve strength and flexibility. I've also used the balance ball as a chair while watching TV or while working at my desk. It still strengthens and tones the abs and you can't keep from rolling around on it because, well, it is fun!

If you like yoga moves or Pilates, do the basics. Try some bridge, cobra, plank, down dog, pigeon, and frog poses. I would recommend taking a few yoga or Pilates classes first, however, because learning proper positioning is key. I have found group classes as cheap as $10 for a one-hour session, so you don't need to spend a fortune. You should also get a yoga mat, especially if you only have hardwood floors at home. A yoga kit will come with instructions or a video that can help you learn more about yoga too.

If you are good at picking up on things on your own, there are tons of different books on yoga from which you can learn. Styles and poses differ from all over the world. Hindu-based yoga is different from some of the Korean techniques, for example, so shop around, look at different books and videos, and find one or two that seem to suit you the most and try them. I've seen all sorts of books on yoga: *Yoga for Wimps* and

Yoga for Sex; recently I even saw *Barbar's Yoga Book for Elephants* (the kind with a trunk and not really fat people).

Once you have learned a few moves, choreographing them into a set of movements leading one into the other and then repeating the entire routine several times keeps things more fun. I change my routine each time, so as not to get bored and to keep working different muscle groups.

Remember to breathe in when you contract the muscles and exhale when you extend.

Warm Muscles Are Happy Muscles

When you are ready to "have at it" and you're jogging everywhere you go, don't forget to start with stretching exercises for about five minutes, like the ones with which you should start your day. When we start to work out, our bodies need more oxygen, so our heart rates increase, sending the oxygen to the working muscles. The heart needs time to respond to this increase in activity, especially if its biggest demand recently has been using the TV remote. By stretching before engaging in more aerobic activity, you give your heart a chance to get going and you are less likely to suffer injuries to your muscles, tendons, and/or joints. You should also be able to work out longer at a higher intensity and burn more calories if your muscles aren't prematurely fatigued or in pain. Warming up also helps prevent colds and flu because it counters the stress hormones that are released during aerobics.

Good Stretches

Arms and Shoulders:

- ✔ Bend triceps back behind your head and then across your chest. Use the other arm to add tension and gently pull at the elbow.
- ✔ Reach your arms straight out to the side and roll in circles clockwise and then counterclockwise.
- ✔ Roll your shoulders forward and back.
- ✔ Interlock your fingers behind you and pull your arms upward. Hold for 10 to 15 seconds.

- ✔ Position arms in a T. Keep them level with your shoulders and pinch them back. Hold as long as you can!

Neck:

- ✔ Release stored tension by dropping your right ear to your right shoulder, then reach up with your right hand and let the weight of your arm add to the stretch. Switch sides.
- ✔ Make circles with your head slowly in one direction and then in the other.

Legs and Butt:

- ✔ While standing, do lunges by staggering your stance, one leg back and dip down with the knee. Switch sides.
- ✔ From a seated, leaning-back position on the floor, lift your legs slowly. Stretch your legs forward in front of you and tug back on your toes with your fingers. Roll onto each side and lift each leg, keeping knees firm. Stand up and stretch your quadriceps by grasping your ankle and bending your leg back to your butt. Switch sides. This exercise is also good for balance.
- ✔ While sitting on the floor, stretch one leg in front, bring the other foot to the side of the knee; bend forward with a straight back. Alternate sides. Then try a butterfly pose stretch by bringing your feet together.
- ✔ Remember the "peeing poodle from aerobics in the '80s"? Get down on all fours and lift your leg then alternate sides. Do a 10-count for three repetitions. Then kick straight back and up for the same count.
- ✔ While lying on your back, knees bent, lift off the floor one vertebra at a time into a bridge pose. You can make this exercise more challenging by lifting your arms over your head or extending one leg then the other, keeping knees level. If you need more support, place your hands under your buttocks.
- ✔ Work the calves by standing with your feet hip width apart.

Spread your toes flat on the ground and raise up onto your toes. Do 20 repetitions nice and slow.

Abdominal and Obliques:

- ✔ Do crunch-style sit-ups by lying on the floor with your knees bent, hands behind your head, and then slowly come halfway up. If you can easily do 50, make it more challenging by shifting your knees to the floor on each side or off the ground, holding them at a right angle, then do your crunches. Do bicycle crunches by alternating knees to elbows.
- ✔ Use a balance ball. Balance balls usually come with videos or charts that teach you how to use them. Balance balls are great ways to stretch muscles and feel youthful all at the same time. What more of an incentive do you need?
- ✔ Gyms offer classes that focus primarily on the abdominals, so if you really want to tone your belly flab, you may want to take a class.

Back:

- ✔ Lie on your stomach hands under your shoulders, keeping elbows bent; lift head and chest into a cobra pose.
- ✔ Lie on stomach and reach with each hand for each ankle, lift arms and legs off of the floor and balance on your pelvis. You are in bow pose.

Total Body:

- ✔ Lie on your stomach, roll your toes under, place elbows under shoulders, clasp hands tighten abdominal muscles, and lift. Hold for one minute or as long as you can. You are in a plank pose.
- ✔ Lie on your stomach, press hands and feet into the floor; push buttocks into the air, extending arms and legs. You are in down dog pose. Try to drop heals to the floor. You can alternate bending at the knee.

See the Flexibility Chart of the following page to help you learn some of these positions and poses.

FLEXIBILITY CHART:

Lower-Body Squats

Poodle

Sit-Ups

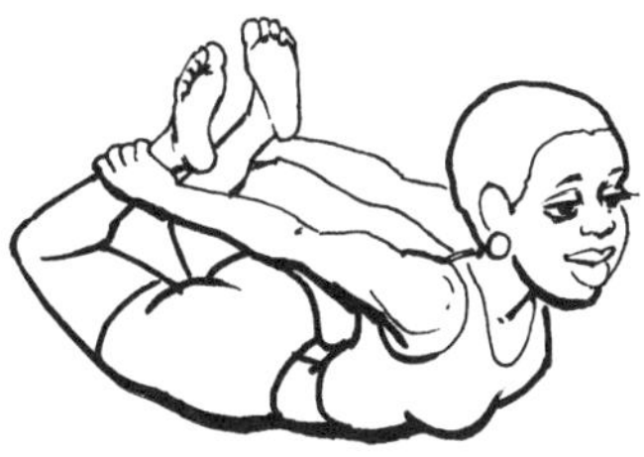

Bow

Add your own notes on your favorite stretches:

- ✔
- ✔
- ✔
- ✔
- ✔
- ✔
- ✔
- ✔

Add Strength Training

Strength training is an important aspect of a total body workout along with cardio and flexibility training. When you build muscle, you will increase your metabolism since muscle burns more calories than fat; by building muscle, you will lose weight. Strength training can also be helpful if you suffer from chronic pain conditions, such as fibromyalgia.

You can begin strength training by adding lighter weights, such as three to five pounds; later, if you feel up to it and want to increase resistance and muscle strength, increase to eight- to ten-pound weights. Do a 10-count *slowly* and then repeat three to five times. Working faster decreases benefits when it comes to weight training because you are relying on the velocity of the motion rather than on your own strength to lift and lower the weight. Keep the motion slow and steady, and stay focused on your form. To avoid muscle injury and to keep from dropping them on your toes, don't jerk the weights up and down.

Wait till about six weeks after beginning strength training to increase your training session to make sure you don't overstress your muscles. Add enough weight so that the resistance is more challenging, but if you tire too fast, you might have added too much at once. Take it in strides; add one, three, or five pounds instead of ten all at once. Add repetitions until you feel fatigued and then do a few more.

If you have joined a gym, you may want to start with the *weight machines* since they are easier to use than dumbbells and barbells. The machines have guidelines pasted right on them to follow along with, and trainers can teach you proper positioning and stance. The machines are adjustable to fit your body's height, and of course you can add to or reduce the amount of weight you actually lift. You don't have to worry about dropping an eight-pound dumbbell on your big toe in front of spandex Ken and Barbie, and it is easier to maintain proper form using the machines. Some gyms even have dual hydraulic machines that are resistance based. There are no weights to deal with and there is less chance for injury or muscle strain because you are using your own body's strength to push up and pull back. (Curves has these types of machines designed especially for women.) Good gyms have a wide variety of machines that target key muscle groups, and you can work upper or lower body muscles. The variety of machines will keep you from getting bored. You can mix up your weightlifting sessions and target different areas of your body, especially the jiggle spots.

If you feel ready to take on the testosterone-laden weight room, make sure also to get a trainer who will help you select the right weights to lift and teach you the proper technique. Again, slower is better (isn't that true for almost everything?), and proper posture is key. Most fitness centers post charts that can teach you different lifts and how to target different muscle groups. Look for strength training pointers in health and fitness magazines as well.

When lifting weights, concentrate on either the upper or the lower body during a particular session. According to one of the trainers I have worked with at Fitness First, strength training is most beneficial when energy is concentrated in one area of the body to burn the most fat. So, if you are working on your arms, just do arms. Don't do legs or you will lessen the fat burned from your arm muscles, and it will take longer to get rid of the jiggle. (The same goes for when you are doing legs.) Therefore, it is best to alternate strength training session activities and be more targeted.

If you have gotten weights to work out with at home, make sure someone who knows what they are talking about has shown you how to use them. Remember to start off slowly so as not to cause injury. Do repetitions of ten and then increase weekly or monthly. But don't overdo it, unless you desire to have arms like Stallone. You do need lean muscles to help your body burn more fat calories, and arms that don't jiggle make you look younger too!

You may want to keep track and log your progress. At Fitness First, as at most centers, there are workout cards for members to track their sessions and monitor their progress. If you don't join a gym, you may want to consider monitoring your progress on your own with one of those free calendars you got at your last clinic appointment or in your own log book. Use the following Strength Training Chart as an example to set up your own log.

By the way, don't panic if you get on the scale and have gained a few pounds. If you have been doing a lot of weightlifting, you will be building muscle, and muscle tissues weighs more than fat. But building muscle will help you burn fat and lose more weight in the long run.

Chart Your Strength Training

Use the chart on the following page to monitor your progress when using weights. Keep track of how many weeks go by at the same weight and any increases in weight you may make. Make sure to alternate the parts of your body that you are targeting to optimize your caloric burn and toning. Make notations if you have had any injuries or pain during a workout and see how long it takes to heal. Contact a doctor if pain persists for more than a few days.

STRENGTH TRAINING CHART			
Target Area	Date	Weight lifted Machine	Comments
Abdominal			
Obliques			
Arms			
Shoulders			
Legs			
Back			

Type Casting

Do you know your body type? This was something that I found interesting, as I was researching what works/what doesn't work for improving my health. In the 1940s psychologist William Sheldon documented that there were three different body types. (He was trying to connect body shape to personality, but that didn't work.) However, his discovery did help dietitians and physical therapists develop exercise programs.

The three body types are:

- ✔ *Ectomorphs* have long and lean muscles and are extremely flexible.
- ✔ *Endomorphs* are round or have pear-shaped bodies (like me!)
- ✔ *Mesomorphs* have a muscular build.

Experts say that you can maximize your exercise training potential by targeting your routine to your body's muscle type. Ectomorphs need the most cross-training and muscle toning to help add shape, although they will probably find flexibility training the most fun. Endomorphs need to do more endurance and low-impact exercises to help burn the extra fat. Upper-body strength training can help balance out shape. Mesomorphs should stick to aerobics and flexibility training, but be careful not to overdo it with weights, unless they really want to bulk up.

Regardless of your body type, it is always important to cross-train for your overall health. Knowing your body type will help you focus on how to best expend your energy in the areas you need to target most, but doing cardio, flexibility, and strength training is important to maximizing your body's overall functioning.

Kegel

In yoga class, my instructor describes the Kegel move in this way: It is the muscle contraction that occurs when you are in the middle of peeing in the bathroom and the phone rings, and you stop to jump up to answer it. Kegeling is a technique developed by Dr. Arnold Kegel to treat urinary incontinence or overactive bladder syndrome. The exercise has become a popular move among yoga instructors because when you contract the muscles in your pelvis floor, you are improving your posture and are working the surrounding muscle groups. It is important to Kegel when you are doing stretches, especially abdominal ones, or lifting weights.

And, as you can guess, the girls on *Sex and the City* practice Kegeling because it is also known to improve orgasms for women and their partner. If you Kegel during sex, you will have more control and intensity with orgasms. So it is a skill that can come in handy!

By the by, men can also Kegel to improve their workout and to become better sexual partners.

To Gym or Not to Gym

It can be difficult to decide whether to join a gym, fitness center, health club, or spa. Joining involves a financial and time commitment, as well as a willingness to be seen in public in spandex, which you may not be ready to do early on in your workout routine. As I mentioned earlier, it took me over a year and lots of lost pounds before I felt ready to be one of those people who went running off to their health club, but now I really enjoy it. I have learned a great deal from the trainers and class instructors at Fitness First regarding technique, form, and intensity for whatever type of workout I am doing. I have also met friends there who share some of the same struggles. We can talk and laugh for hours after a class about the different diets and exercises we have tried. Knowing that someone is going to be waiting for me at a class helps motivate me to get there.

If you are thinking about joining a fitness center, figure out what is right for you.

Things to consider:

- ✔ **Location:** How easily can you get there? Fitness First is two minutes from my house, which was a primary factor. I knew if it were too far, I would never drag myself there.
- ✔ **Hours:** Is it open hours that work for you? What are the class schedules? Scheduled classes are a good way to keep going to the gym because they start at a specific time and you are forced to put them into your schedule, which I think is a very important tip.

- ✔ **Atmosphere:** I wanted simple. I don't like the over-the-top froufrou or too much glitz. Fitness First, a local chain primarily in the Maryland and Virginia area, doesn't have all of the amenities, but the layout of the place works for me and it is close to my home, which was the most important factor for me.
- ✔ **Cleanliness:** Does the place seem sanitary or smell like an old locker room? Lots of people are sweating on the same equipment you will be using; is there a policy and supplies to wipe down the equipment after each use?
- ✔ **Amenities:** What is the locker room like? Is there a sauna, hot tub, or pool? Are there tennis or racquetball courts? Is there a juice bar? Is there a massage therapist on the premises? What would make this a fulfilling experience for you?
- ✔ **People:** Are the trainers helpful and are the class instructors good? Is it spandex city with Ken and Barbie, or do you feel comfortable? Does it matter if it is coed? I have made some friends at the gym, and that has been a bonus.
- ✔ **Cost:** Is it affordable? What kind of payment plans or discounts does the gym offer? Is there a sign-up fee? Can you pay month to month, or do you have to sign a yearly contract? What is the cancellation and refund policy?
- ✔ **Children:** Does the gym offer childcare while you work out? Does it have programs for children?

You may want to ask about a *trial membership period* or go as a guest with someone who already belongs to a health club. Joining a friend's club might help you get there more often. You may also want to know about using gyms in other locations if you go on a trip or putting a membership on hold for medical or other reasons when you will not be able to go for extended periods of time.

Another point to consider is that some clubs are part of a huge chain operation; for example, Bally's and Gold's Gym have thousands of clubs worldwide. They may be owned and operated by different individuals, but they follow the policies and procedures of the overall franchise. There are health clubs that are owned by a single owner, who may have one club or several locations; as in the case of Fitness First—there are about a dozen. There are advantages and disadvantages to joining either type. A franchise club offers the possibility of working out in other facilities when you travel or transferring your membership if you move. A single-owner facility may have more flexibility with pricing and cancellation policies. Some of these clubs are more likely to let you work out and pay a daily fee ranging from $8 to $15 than are the larger franchises. You may also want to check out what is available through your city or county. Community recreational centers or the YMCA or YWCA might be more affordable. There is also Jazzercise, where you can pay as you go.

To learn more about selecting a health clubs, look on the Internet at *www.HealthClubs.com* or see the International Health, Racquet, and Sportsclub Association (IHRSA) at *www.ihrsa.org*. This large trade association educates club owners and managers on how to best run a facility and has information on legal and legislative issues.

If you choose not to join a gym, then what?

If you decide against joining a health club, you still need to develop some sort of an exercise schedule or program for yourself. If you are a self-starter, you may want to consider home videos. I would suggest investing in several different types so you don't get bored and quit. You should also make sure to get an array of videos that give you a total body workout. Get a yoga or Pilates video or DVD, a weight training video, and one that is more aerobic or a series that offers flexibility, strength, and aerobic activity. Another option is to invest in home equipment. Since this can be expensive, make sure it is right for you. If you buy a stationary bike, for example, make sure it is appropriate for your size and has features that will allow you to make it more challenging as your ability increases. Also, make sure the equipment will fit in your home and won't be an eyesore. If you hide it in a dank basement with clutter, poor lighting, and poor circulation, you are not as likely to use it. It will just become another item in storage. If you are going to bring exercise equipment into your home, make sure it fits in and that you can create an atmosphere conducive to working out. It has to be in a place where you want to spend time, play music or the TV, has good lighting and fresh air. If your space is limited, then find smaller types of equipment, such as an exercise ball, yoga mat, or other body toner. Look for products made by Livingarts (*www.gaiam.com*) Kathy Smith, or Denise Austin Signature Series made by Terra Star (*www.terrastar.net*). (You can also watch Denise Austin on weekday mornings on Lifetime TV.) These products are more compact, so you can even travel with them, and they come with instructional videos, CDs, or DVDs—make sure you have the players needed to watch or listen to the instructions!

Real Women Have Curves for Women

I wish I had known about Curves for Women three years ago when I first began my search for a healthier lifestyle. Curves is a 30-minute total body workout that you do a minimum of three times a week to achieve weight loss and muscle-toning goals. It is done in a circuit that consists of exercise machines that are based on dual hydraulic resistance and recovery stations. The machines work every major muscle group when you push forward with one muscle group and pull back with the opposing set. The recovery stations allow the muscles to rest between sets, but still keep you at your target heart rate. Depending on your fitness level, you can do the recovery stations by marching in place or by twisting to the music. Every 30 seconds a voiceover announces, "Change stations now," and you move onto the next machine or platform. After three rounds on the circuit, 30 minutes has gone by. As part of a cool-down, a chart takes you through a series of stretches, which are yoga poses, until you are done. There is no muss or fuss with weights, no class schedules to be on time for, and no mirrors or men! Once your learn the proper form for each of the machines, you are ready to begin. Fitness technicians help and monitor the circuit continuously. They will also measure and weigh you each month so that you can see your progress. The music is great. It is a lot of fun, and the mutual support from the women is uplifting.

There is also a Curves Weight Loss Plan that you can follow on your own. You complete a self-test to determine if you should follow a Calories Sensitive Diet or a Carbohydrate Sensitive Diet. There are meal plans, grocery lists, and recipes that will help meet your goals. To find a Curves near you, check the website at *www.curvesinternational.com*.

Train with a Trainer

If you belong to a gym, ask the owner, manager, or fitness director about the club's training and certification requirements. There are several levels of certification available. Some trainers have taken a 500-hour Personal Fitness Trainer (PFT) certificate course that meets state and professional organization requirements. A Certified Personal Trainer (CPT) has taken a basic one- or two-day course and continuing education units. For a more intense level of athletic training, you may want to look for a Certified Athletic Trainer (CAT), who has met the requirements set by the National Athletic Trainers' Association Board of Certification (NATABOC). To become a CAT, a trainer must have a bachelor's degree in physical education or in an associated field, have been supervised, and have passed the NATABOC exam. CATs primarily work with athletes and teams.

To find out more about locating a CPT or a CAT, contact the National Athletic Trainers' Association at *www.nata.org*. I have found two good sources on the Internet that will help you locate a PFT: the American Council on Exercise at *www.ace.org* and the National Academy of Sports Medicine at *www.nasm.org*. You can search for a trainer by zip code at both of these sites. Information also is available from the American Aerobic Association/International Sports Medicine Association at *www.aaai-ismafitness.com*. If you have never done any endurance or strength training before, definitely start with a trainer and have someone who is qualified develop a program for you that will help you avoid injury and maximize your benefits.

When selecting a personal fitness trainer, check out their credentials, match their specialty areas to your needs (i.e.; weightlifting, senior health, youth, athletes, etc), discuss your health concerns, injuries, or any limitations, and make sure you feel comfortable with him or her physically and emotionally. Trust your instincts. If you don't feel as if the person is listening to you, find someone else. After I had arthroscopic knee surgery for a torn meniscus, I worked with Mike, a trainer at Fitness First, whom I felt comfortable with and who pushed me enough to get me back on my feet again without me ever feeling unsafe. I didn't have the same comfort level (real or imagined) with other trainers, so I only booked sessions with Mike. Mike listened to my concerns, talked me through the exercises, and remembered where we were from session to session. He helped me keep up my routine. When I started working out on my own again, I felt confident that I knew what I was doing and that I could increase my weight-bearing exercises and repetitions without injury. Despite the fact that I was off of my feet for several months, I did not regain any weight during that time and in fact continued to lose.

Keep It Simple

No matter what type of activity it is, find something you think you might like to do and try it. Add new things as you feel you can. You don't need to rush out and buy every abdo-buster advertised on TV to be working out. Walking, jogging, running, hiking, stretching, and lawn mowing are all free (provided you already own a lawn mower) and don't need big investments. Do wear the proper shoes though. (See *An Excuse to Buy Shoes* tip.)

Once you have found an activity you feel committed to, then look into making the big purchase. If you have gone on a few bike trips or kayaking where you have rented or borrowed equipment, but now are ready to become the champion kayaker of the universe, then investigate the different options and buy what is right for you. Check out product information online and visit several stores before you buy any expensive items. You want to be sure that what you invest in is right for your height, weight, and skill level. If you purchase an item that requires more skill than you have, it will end up on a rack in the garage or under a pile of old blankets in the basement. It would be better to buy an easier-to-use model, then trade up when your skills improve and if your commitment has remained strong. You can always sell the old one. You can also buy a used one from someone who has been at it longer and is trading up. Many sports clubs and associations have bulletin boards where "for sale" items are posted. Check those out as well, it you want to save some money, but remember, buyer beware!

Drivercises

Have you been known to develop road rage while behind the wheel? Have you yelled at other drivers or muttered curses to yourself? Well, instead of thinking about the idiot on his cell phone in the Land Rover who just cut you off, try these moves:

- ✔ Hold onto the steering wheel with both hands as if you were back in driver's education, sit up straight and contract your abdomen muscles away from your seat belt, and Kegel. Hold and repeat. Breathe in on contractions and breathe out when releasing. Do the same thing with your butt.

- ✔ Red light? Grab hold of your headrest behind you with both hands, push your elbows out to the side, and pull back, expanding your chest on an inhale at the same time, hold, and wait for the light to turn green and release.

- ✔ Traffic jammed up for miles? Try rotating your head in slow circles, keeping your eyes forward (for obvious reasons). Also slowly flex your neck from side to side. Add to the stretch by using your opposite hand to gently push your head toward your shoulder. Switch sides.

- ✔ Roll your shoulders forward in a slow circular motion and then backward.

- ✔ Breathe deeply and sigh out loud: AAAHHH!

Please do your best not to be an aggressive driver. It is not good for your stress level or mine, especially if you cause an accident. Practice the *Self-Talk* tip techniques described in the *Stress Management* section and know that a few minutes late here or there is not really so awful in the scheme of things. If you can't give yourself more time to get there, then just give in and relax!

Desk Busters

Most of the drivercises can also be done from a desk while at work. You can push back from your desk for a moment and stretch out your arms and legs. Touch your toes and reach for the ceiling for a count of 20. Flex your heels and toes and stretch out your fingers. Go and walk up and down the stairs purposefully. Take an exercise ball to the office and use it instead of a desk chair. It will keep you rolling! Try a quick relaxation exercise (see *Relaxation Tips*) with deep breathing to clear your mind.

If you don't have your own office, find an empty conference room or a break room and stretch out in there. Or, better yet, go to the park across the street for a few flexibility moves. Find a bench and use a relaxation technique.

These are better ways to take a break and reenergize yourself than by heading off to the vending machine or out for a cigarette. You will get your blood flow going and elevate your heart rate, which will make you feel more pumped up than a candy bar or a smoke will. Short bursts of cardio exercise can be an important break in your day because it will speed up your metabolism and decrease your appetite.

Step It Up

Take the stairs. If up is too much, start with down. Add one flight at a time on the ups until you can handle several flights at once. People spend a lot of money to take step classes in the health clubs, but you can do if for free at work and you don't have to wear spandex or listen to Michael Jackson music. If you work in an office building, deliver the memo on the J.Lo website ban to your colleague working two floors above by dropping it off in person rather than sending it through the inner-office mail.

Why waste all that time waiting to get where you are going on an elevator? Think about this: You just drove like a maniac to get to your desired destination, weaving through traffic and darting around corners, to just stand there and *wait* patiently for the elevator! I say, "No way!" Burn off all your road rage on the staircase. But a word of caution: *Don't use stairways that don't seem safe and secure*, such as a parking garage at midnight. (Remember the rape scene with the psychiatrist in the parking garage stairwell in the HBO series *The Sopranos*?) When you use stairwells, make sure they are well lit and well traveled.

Elevator Lifts

You've got to go to the 29th floor and you're wearing high heels or the stairwell is dimly lit? Not a good time to take the stairs, so take the elevator and use the ride to flex your legs, heels, and toes. Stretch out your arms or press your back against the wall and pretend to sit, and then hold that position for as long as you can or until you get to your floor. If other people get on the elevator, add a yawn, so they will think you have just come from a very boring meeting and are not delusional about a chair.

You can lift up onto your toes and stretch out your calf muscles if you don't want to look as obvious. You can also use this time to stretch your biceps and triceps by dropping your hand between your shoulders and gently tugging back on your elbow or clasping your hands together behind your back, rolling your shoulder blades together, and lifting up your hands.

Park and Go

While looking for a parking space is another good time to consider your road rage level. You've just driven wildly to get to the store before it closes or they sell the last Chia pet you were going to get your Aunt Ethel for her birthday. Now the place is packed and there is nowhere to park. You can save time circling around the parking lot looking for a space by simply going to the back of the lot first, parking there, and briskly walking to the store. An added incentive is that you will also save your car from door dings. Also, remember to keep it safe and park by a light.

Don't Forget to Breathe

You can go weeks without eating and days without drinking, but you would die if you went minutes without breathing. We spend lots of time thinking, planning, and preparing to eat and drink, but we don't think much at all about breathing. Breathing does not involve much of a thought process; for those of us who have difficulty walking and chewing gum, this is a good thing. If I had to think about every breath I drew, not much else would get accomplished. However, in my yoga class I have learned a lot about breathing and how important it is during cardio, flexibility, and strength training, as well as during meditation.

For the most part, most people tend to breathe very shallowly from the upper part of the lungs and don't move the oxygen and carbon dioxide in and out the way they should. (I am very guilty of this myself, just ask my mother.) Breathing should really be done from deep in the diaphragm or from the belly. The other mistake I have made over and over again while exercising is holding my breath. Lots of people do this; it's probably why instructors from yoga to aerobics are always yelling, "Don't forget to breathe!"

You will notice that many of the exercise and the relaxation techniques described in this book involve breathing with inhalation/exhalation timing. Take a moment to make sure you know how to breathe. Put one hand on your chest and the other just above your pelvis. Breathe in slowly and feel your chest cavity expand. Continue to breathe in until you feel as if your lungs will burst like a balloon, and then exhale slowly. This is the way you should breathe when you are lifting weights, doing stomach crunches, coming in and out of yoga poses, or practicing relaxation during a meditation. This will also help you slow down your timing and not rush through your repetitions.

Asthma, allergies, and other pulmonary disorders are on the rise in this nation, affecting an estimated 50 million Americans (like me). More and more people are using inhalers and other medication. I once thought I was the odd one with an inhaler in my handbag, but now I see more and more people with them. I guess pollution has caught up with most of us, but anyone can be diagnosed with asthma at any point in his or her life. It is important to take care of your respiratory system and practice proper breathing, just as you would exercise any other part of your body.

The breathing techniques I have learned in my yoga class have really helped my breathing, not just when I am working out, but all of the time. If you have asthma or some other pulmonary condition, I recommend that you at least try yoga. Let the yoga instructor know about your particular condition. If you are under a doctor's care for a chronic lung condition, discuss the benefits of yoga with him or her prior to engaging in anything too strenuous.

An Excuse to Buy Shoes

This is the tip you have been waiting for, the one that involves shoe shopping as part of your exercise routine. OK, I am not talking about the really cute pair of stiletto Ferragamos, but the right sneaker can be very important for the activity you choose. There are all kinds of sneakers for running, walking, tennis, basketball, hiking, cross-training, and so on. Figure out what activity (or activities) you want to do and get the shoe for that intensity. Make sure the shoe fits. Get someone who knows how to pick and fit a sneaker to help you. I definitely advise you to invest money in proper footwear when you begin to exercise. A blood blister on my *left* foot convinced me to get the *right* sneaker.

Don't forget that mall walking counts as exercise too. Compare different stores, sales, brands, and selections before purchasing. Remember you can also walk to the mall or at least park in the back of the parking lot and walk to the front door. It all counts!

P.S.: A New Use for Vaseline

We all know what a great lubricant Vaseline can be; but if you really want to avoid blisters, use it on your feet before you go out for a long walk or jog off into the sunset. Spread some on the soles of your feet and by your toes before putting on your socks and shoes. My nurse friend, Jane, taught me this one, and it has really helped.

And a Sports Bra

And, ladies, while you are mall walking, get that sports bra. A sports bra is a good idea, especially if you are forever grateful to the creator of under-wire. After exercising you can become sore in places you would never have guessed. You can damage breast tissue if you are not properly supported and end up with more sag and less tone in spite of the exercising you are doing. For proper fit, lean over and lift into a bra. Don't smash! A bra is too tight if flesh is popping out of the sides and too big if there is still a lot of bounce.

INSPIRATION TIPS

To me, feeling inspired is the most important part of healthy living and makes the mind-body-spirit connection work. The things that inspire us and keep us going are what life is really all about. For some people, it is their faith in God, their family, their art, or their own sense of wonder. When we nourish our spirit, we can do almost anything. Sometimes the hardest part is recognizing our muses and knowing how and when to use them. Inspirational sources covers everything from family, friends, heroes, work, hobbies, habits, interests, pets, entertainment choices (music, poetry, theater, etc.), religious and community activities, volunteerism, idealism, education, travel, and sex. Did I forget anything? Oh, yes, food! See, it's working already!

I have learned that finding the things that help me feel good about myself and what I am doing helps keep me motivated. You know how some things stick in your head like words from an old song that you can't seem to forget? Then there are the things that play over and over again in your head (very often using your mother's voice, pitch, and frequency) that are actually inspiring.

The thing that sticks in my head and helps keep me focused is the quote I used over 20 years ago in my high school yearbook when I was trying to be sophisticated: "*To thine own self be true and as night follows day, thou canst be false to any man.*" William Shakespeare wrote that *way* before I did, but for some reason it's the little voice that plays in my head whenever I am trying to make a stressful decision. Going with my gut may not have always been the best thing to do at the time (my mouth has gotten me in trouble a few times) but I could always live with myself later. I have also found inspiration in my sense of spirituality, my friendships and relationships with others, and my dog.

Why is feeling inspired important to weight loss? Without sounding too Zen guru-ish, I believe there is a mind-body-spirit connection. How we feel about ourselves, and what we are doing will influence how we treat ourselves emotionally and our bodies physically. We should be consistent in how we think, feel, and act in order for our lives to have balance and tranquility. Therefore, if we want to live a healthier lifestyle, it is important to inventory the inspirations in our lives and not just the food on our shelves. This is where taking care of your spirit comes into play. I have given you my examples, what are yours?

What inspires you?

- ✔
- ✔
- ✔
- ✔
- ✔
- ✔
- ✔
- ✔

The following tips include the inspirations that I have used to help keep me motivated and on a positive track in living a healthy lifestyle.

Attitude Is Everything

Your greatest source of inspiration should be yourself. In order to make any lifestyle changes, you must believe in yourself, be objective about your needs, and be able to set realistic goals. If you can't convince yourself that you are worth the effort, then no one can and none of the tips in this book or anywhere else are going to be of help to you. Go back to the "Your Story" section and review what you wrote about yourself and your goals. Are they realistic?

Most of us tend to be our own harshest critics. I have sat with absolutely gorgeous women and men who can pick apart their every flaw. They see their every wrinkle and every fat molecule, which they believe everyone else is viewing with a microscope. We all do this. I know I could tell you about every hair that I can't manage, the cellulite on my thighs, and the circles under my eyes that can shine through any amount of concealer depending on how the light hits my face. But none of this self-loathing or self-deprecation is helpful in improving your health or to losing weight.

If you truly are going to make healthful living changes, you have to see yourself in a positive light first, no matter how much you weigh. If you are negative about yourself, how are you going to accomplish anything? I know I have had the most successes in my life when I have been pumped up and ready to take on the world. If you take a moment to think back over your life and reflect on your successes, wasn't your attitude key to getting you what you wanted? You need to think about your health in the same way. You need to be able to keep positive affirmations about yourself in your daily thought process.

Repeat the following affirmations as you get dressed every morning:

- ✔ **I am loved!**
- ✔ **I look good!**
- ✔ **I am worth it!**
- ✔ **I can do it!**
- ✔ **I am sexy!**
- ✔ **I don't need to put junk in my body to feel good.**
- ✔ **Look out, world, here I come!**

Maybe that last one is a bit over the top, but you get the idea. Did you say them out loud? If you didn't, go back now and shout them out!

When we love, we need to do it unconditionally to make relationships work, but we often forget to start with ourselves. It is how we feel about ourselves that makes the difference in how we face the world and our challenges. See the glass as half full, and it will be. If your attitude about yourself, your life, and the world you live in is positive, you are more likely to have positive outcomes in the things you do. If you are pessimistic and defeatist, then you will quit before you get what you want. This is true not just for weight loss, but for life in general.

It may seem contradictory to say that you should feel good about yourself even when you weigh 220 pounds and are trying to lose weight, but if you can't start by treating yourself right when you are overweight, what makes you think that you will be able to treat yourself any better when you weigh 130 pounds? Losing the weight really won't make a difference in your life if you still don't feel good about yourself. Your attitude about yourself is what allowed you to gain the extra weight in the first place. Start on a new footing. Forgive yourself for all past sins (and the ones you are going to commit next week), and pledge to treat yourself better. Who deserves your love more than you do? Now give yourself a hug and take the following pledge!

I will forgive myself for all my past mistakes and errors in judgment. I cannot change those things, but I will learn from them and try not to behave the same way again. I will not punish myself for the mistakes I make in the future, but will look for the opportunities to learn and live a healthy life.

____

Your Signature

Now start on a new page in your life and remember this pledge you made to yourself. Cut it out and hang it up on the refrigerator if you need the visual reminder.

Positive People Power

The people who care about you the most can be another great source of inspiration. The friends and family who have gone hiking, bought tofu, and made me laugh are keepers! They have helped me stay motivated and commiserated with me along the way. As I have mentioned, I have a group of female friends—we call ourselves the Guacamole Club. When the club meets, we first make guacamole (hence the name of the club). We have also been known to make frozen margaritas, but mostly we talk about our lives, loves, and work. We problem-solve together and laugh our asses off! The women in the club have been among my greatest supporters and cheering section, not just for losing weight but for living. These are the types of folks you need in your life. The ones who are only around to talk about their problems, are negative about themselves and what you are trying to accomplish, and are dull, uninteresting, and taxing to be around, need to go. You know who these people are: a high school buddy who has been in your life way too long, a relative who always needs a favor, a coworker who feels compelled to share every intimate detail of her life, a controlling manipulative lover—Bye-bye! You may not realize it, but they zap you of your energy and take away your time from things you would rather be doing or people you would rather be with. You are left frustrated and hurrying through other things. Not only is this poor time management, but it also adds to your stress. (See more on this in the tips on dealing with stress.) Of course, there are some people you have to deal with—a boss or your children—but take a moment to think about who is in your life and if they are a positive force or a drain on your energy.

Do you have more positive people or energy zappers in your life? Now think about how much time you spend with each group. Do you wish you were spending more time with the people who you enjoy? Are the zappers winning out? I am going to save you a lot of money and therapy hours by telling you this: If you have convinced yourself that they can't live without you, you're wrong! They *can* live without you, and they *will* solve their own problems. Spend more time on yourself and you will feel better about who you are. Get rid of all that negative energy: if you are honest with yourself, you don't trust these people and they don't make you feel good about yourself.

Use the following chart to list Positive People and Energy Zappers. Which list is longer? If there are more zappers on your list than positive

Positive People	Energy Zappers

people, you have just identified a major problem in your life: You are living for everyone else. Change this around or at least find more balance. See the section on positive people/positive time plan under the *Stress Management* tips to help improve the positive forces in your life.

Volunteer

I know how busy you are, but before you skip this tip, think about the puppies you've always dreamed of saving or the nightmares you've had about global warming. You have secretly believed that the rain forest needs you. The sick children at the local hospice you've read about in the newspaper have touched your heart. Healthy living is not just about taking care of your physical self. It helps to also think about your emotional and spiritual side, and the best way to take care of those needs is to get involved with a cause that makes you feel like you are doing something worthwhile. National, state, and local nonprofit agencies, civic/veteran associations, and religious organizations always need more help than they have staff and may need your expertise or just a pair of hands to get a job done. This does not mean you have to give up all of your worldly possessions and trek up a Tibetan mountain, but how about:

- ✔ Spending a few hours at your local community or veteran's hospital (see if your employer has a program that will let you use company time volunteering)
- ✔ Reading to children at your local library or after-school program
- ✔ Teaching teens about your profession by calling schools and offering to visit classes.
- ✔ Training with the Red Cross or the Salvation Army to be able to deploy during a natural disaster
- ✔ Offering pro bono services to a community agency if you have a needed skill (legal, medical, secretarial, accounting, cooking,

sewing, teaching, coaching, counseling, painting, care-giving, gardening, acting, building, cleaning, horsemanship, writing, clowning, dancing … what else can you do?)

- ✔ Donating clothes to a women's shelter, especially business suits that can help homeless women dress appropriately to get jobs
- ✔ Food shopping for a family involved with a home hospice program
- ✔ Contributing to a food bank and serving meals
- ✔ Writing press releases for the community center
- ✔ Becoming involved with your fire station (Not every volunteer fights fires, but *you can too*!)
- ✔ Finding out about a neighborhood watch program or the Guardian Angels, or offering your services to local police departments
- ✔ Helping out at the humane society or being a "foster parent" to train seeing-eye dogs
- ✔ Joining a community gentrification project or building Houses for Humanity

I have found that the work I have done as a volunteer with nonprofit organizations has been a great way to put myself into a positive frame of mind. In spite of the tragedies I have seen or have heard about as a trauma specialist, I have learned a lot about what is really important in life from those survivors I have been privileged to get to know. I have edited an association newsletter and enjoyed the time I got to spend working with authors to develop their articles and learn about their work all over the United States and in other parts of the world.

Watch your local newspaper for organizations that are looking for volunteers or check your phone directory for the community agencies in your neighborhood. If you call and offer your services, they will more than likely be able to find something for you to do.

Hobbies Aren't Just for Kids

Stamp collecting was all you once thought about, but now your stamp books are covered with dust in your mother's attic. You won't let her throw them out because they are full of memories, but who has time for that kid's stuff anymore, you tell yourself. Sound sort of familiar? Well, maybe not stamps, but there is something of yours in boxes somewhere that you stopped making time for.

As kids we enjoyed hobbies and sports, but now the responsibilities and obligations of adulthood have taken the place of such frivolity. A shelf of Barbie dolls may no longer be what you need, but it is still just as important to have things in your life that make you feel good. Like so many of us, you may have shelved your childhood hobbies without discovering more adult pursuits, which is understandable since the demands of college, jobs, and family have probably entered the pictured. But planning time for you do something that you enjoy and find relaxing (that is not necessarily exercise and diet related) can be just the mental break you need so you don't have a mental break.

If you have time to watch TV, you have time for a hobby, especially one that you can do while watching TV that can replace the overeating that tends to take place in front of the tube. You can learn how to crochet (real easy) or knit, cross-stitch or rug hook while in front of the TV. Engage the family in a 1,000-piece puzzle. Take a low-calorie cooking class at your community center, or take a college course on horticulture. Plant your own vegetable garden so you can enjoy vegetables you grew yourself. Gardening can also be great exercise with all of the tilling, weeding, and watering. Go fishing. Paint. Join a book club. Become a regular at karaoke night. Get on a volleyball team at the YMCA or start one at work.

No matter what activity you find to add to your routine, it will help your mind feel sharper and add to your sense of accomplishment, which are all factors in feeling good about yourself. And when you feel good about yourself, you are less likely to overeat, so maybe you want to call your mother and get that stamp collection back after all.

Mirror, Mirror on the Wall, *Who the Hell Is That?*

There is a lot of talk about *body image* these days, especially concerning how young girls see themselves in relation to the images of beauty around them. We are always comparing ourselves to the latest trends on the catwalks, what our sisters look like, and the coworker with the postage-stamp-size miniskirt. But do we really have a good sense of our own bodies?

Today, when people compliment me on how skinny I am, I never just say "thank you." Instead I say, "I am not skinny, I've lost weight." When I look in the mirror, I see a thinner version of myself, but it is as if when I turn away from the mirror, the pounds magically reappear. When my friend Amy and I went shopping recently, I held up a really cute skirt, and said, "What do you think of this?" Amy's response: "What size is that?" Interestingly enough, I've only known Amy since I've lost weight and all she could see was how huge the skirt looked. Sure enough, when I checked the tag it was a size 16, not the size 4 I currently wear. This made me realized just how trained my eye is when I pick out clothes for myself. My body image still subconsciously is drawn to the size 16 even though it has been a few years since I've actually worn one. I've done this many other times. You would think I would have figured this out by now! But when I shop for myself, I inevitably end up trying on three sizes before the jacket I am contemplating fits properly. Then it usually still takes multiple reassurances from total strangers that it's not too tight, the length is right, and the all-time famous "Does this make me look fat?" question has been exhausted.

I've talked to lots of women about body-image issue. No matter what size they are, they all have the same difficulty in recognizing themselves. Additionally, this phenomenon does not seem to apply to when we lose weight. It also seems to occur as we gain weight too. The images we have of ourselves in our minds don't seem to match the realities of our bodies. We either see ourselves as too fat or too skinny or ignore an unhealthy weight with justifications of our age, child bearing or hormones. My weight gain was gradual, although plateaued at about a size 14 or 16. I was almost 200 pounds and still didn't seem myself as obese. Imagine my shock on the day the dietitian showed me my BMI; it was not just in the overweight range but bordering on obese. I was still dressing stylishly and thought I looked good. I've learned a lot since then, but retraining my eye has been one of the hardest parts.

What is the point of all of this? It is to develop an understanding of your own *body image perceptions and misperceptions.* This is all about how we see ourselves: the good, the bad, and the ugly. Developing an accurate sense of yourself is an important part of being able to make accurate assessments in your overall health and well-being. Remember, your health is really more important than beauty. The healthier you are, the better you will look. Run a check and balance scan on yourself to test your own sense of your body.

✔ **Calculate your BMI.** A healthy range is between 19 and 24. (Use the chart from the *Body Mass, Not Pounds* tip.)

✔ **What are your blood levels?** Are they all normal? If you don't know, make a doctor's appointment to have a physical and find out.

✔ **Ask a trusted confidante for feedback on how you look.** (This would *not* be *your mother!* You won't agree with her opinion anyway. And certainly leave your husband or boyfriend out of this. He will feel like it is a trick question and be afraid to answer truthfully, so spare the guy the panic attack.)

✔ **Go for a makeover and see what the pros do with you!** My sister and I appeared on the cable TV makeover show "Style Court." After I was found guilty, I got a great makeover and learned a valuable lesson about how to maximize on my appearance. You don't have to get on a TV reality show to get a makeover. You can simply work with a cosmetologist (at a makeup counter) and a hair stylist. Personal shoppers who can help you update your wardrobe are available at some department stores.

✔ **Scrutinize your wardrobe.** How many different sizes do you have? How long has it been since you wore a 12? Whatever doesn't fit and is so old and faded that even if it did fit you wouldn't wear it, should go. Get rid of all of the things you don't wear and evaluate what is left. Are you dressing to cover up your sins, or are you accentuating your curves? Do the things you buy for yourself make you feel good, or are they merely functional? I cringe when I think of all of the tops and leggings I bought because they were comfortable. Never mind that they were dowdy and at 30, I looked 70 years old. I've come to learn that I can look and feel sexy and still be comfortable.

✔ **Check out that mirror.** Take a moment and really look yourself over from head to toe. Look at your hairstyle, your face, arms, legs, bust, butt, hips, feet. . . . Do you need a new 'do? When was the last time you used a little lip liner? How old is your bra? These are immediate things you can change to adjust your body image that don't require a long-term plan or expenses.

✔ **Don't take yourself for granted and don't make excuses for not looking or feeling as good as you can.** Evaluate the changes you do need to make, journal them, and set your goals using the space in the *Your Story* section.

Stay in the Present or Shop for Today

Don't put off for tomorrow what you want to do today because you haven't lost weight. Complete self-deprivation is not the way to a healthy lifestyle. Don't bargain with yourself. Let's say you've tried on a dress and it looks great! There is a party coming up and you want to look good (the dress is even on sale), but it's a size 14. Your goal is to wear a 10. Do you buy the dress that fits, or do you buy the 10 for the future?

If you haven't figured this one out by now, you are not catching on to the theme of this book. Go with the 14, feel good about looking good for the upcoming event, and then go shopping for a 10 when that is what will fit! Once you can fit in a 10, the 14 can be worn belted, altered, or consigned, or can become a tax deduction when you donate it to your favorite charity thrift store.

This same rule applies for taking a vacation, dating, or doing something else you would like to do. Don't wait until you've lost weight; treat yourself right, right now! How you feel about yourself should not be conditional. How much you weigh has nothing to do with what you are worth as a person. Stay focused and stay your course. You will eventually lose weight, but you need to have fun in the meantime.

Sex—Have It

The stay-in-the-present rule applies here too. Don't wait for rewards, do it now. Can you think of a better reward than sex? It is the one thing that I know of that beats cheesecake. Do you have to be a size 4 to have an orgasm? I think not. You can be a size 24 and still know how to have a good time in bed. I bet Queen Latifah would have a few words for you here too, girlfriend. But many people avoid intimacy because they are embarrassed about their weight and don't want anyone to see them naked. In most cases, weight is not the issue for a person's partner, but for the person him- or herself. Partners who do not want to be with you sexually because they are offended by your weight, but don't mind you doing the laundry, cooking, and cleaning the toilets, are themselves offensive as people and you should really reevaluate how rewarding the relationship is to you anyway. (See *Positive People/Energy Zappers.*) You may find that the source of your overeating is an attempt to "stuff" ungratified emotions with food and find pleasure in another basic human need. An unloving partner or a relationship that has been allowed to go on too long may be worse than the weight or even the cause of it, but the weight becomes the focal point and the excuse to not be happy. If you lose the deadwood, you may just lose the log roll as well.

However, if you realize your weight is really your own issue, then there are ways to feel sexy and still be a big girl (or boy). The real task here is to discover what makes you feel sexy and share it with your partner. Talk about your feelings and issues. Share your concerns and ask for his or her reassurances. Tell him or her what your needs are.

I am always amazed by women who say, "If he loves me he should know. I shouldn't have to tell him." My response to this is "Are you crazy?" These women obviously don't know a thing about men. These are the same creatures who need to be asked ten times to take out garbage and not leave the toilet seat up. *Men are supposed to figure out the complex workings of a woman's emotions?* I don't think so! This tip will save you a lot of time and money in couple's counseling: Tell him what your fears, anxieties, and needs are in very basic and straightforward language. Identify what he can do to help you, and find out his needs. Oh, and check the toilet seat before you sit down. You may get him to be more emotionally responsive, but I believe (and there must be research somewhere to prove this) that the toilet seat thing is just too complex for men to get.

If you don't have a partner and feel your larger size is what is keeping you from getting involved with someone, think again. Men and women come in all shapes and sizes. The right person is out there, you just need to have the confidence in yourself to get out there and find him or her. A person who wants to be with you wants to be with you not just because of how you look, but also for who you are, your values, and your spirit. Exuding sex appeal is for your own emotional gratification and self-confidence. If you are taking care of yourself, dressing for success, and walking tall, then you will attract the companionship of others who admire your ability to project yourself.

On the flip side, don't judge him too harshly either. There is no Prince Charming. All men will eventually burp like toads in your ear while cuddled up watching TV. (They think this is funny.) Get rid of your images of Sleeping Beauty, Cinderella, and Snow White. You need to realize that in those fantasies planted deep into your subconscious, Prince Charming never actually does a lot of talking (or burping,) but real men do. Stimulate his mind and he will be interested in you.

How do you find ways to turn on the sex appeal with your partner or potential partner when you feel insecure in your own sexiness? I've got some ideas on this subject too.

- ✔ **DRESS WITH SEX APPEAL.** Look at Delta Burke. She has fought the battle of the bulge on and off *publicly* for years, but have you ever seen her when she did not look absolutely glamorous? Get your hair and your nails done, wear makeup, and buy the clothes that make you feel like a winner. If you are walking around all of the time in a sloppy old stained and pilfered sweat suit and a ponytail, you won't feel as sexy as when you wear a pantsuit and have gone to the stylist. I have heard women say they are more comfortable when they wear loose fitting-clothes and no makeup, and to that I say, "Bull." Women and men who walk around looking like slobs project an image that reflects the fact that they have given up on themselves. You may be fooling yourself, but you are not fooling anyone else. You still need to perk it up a bit with some makeup and style. I have seen some great-looking women dressed in fashionable sweats, a nice hair clip, and soft makeup in the mall. It just takes a few of the extra touches to change your self-image and how you carry yourself throughout the day. It does make a difference. You will feel better about yourself if you have taken the time to pamper and primp. This does not mean you need to spend hours and a fortune on clothes and products. Find a few things that add a feeling of zazazoom to your style. If you can't give up the leggings and the sweat pants, make sure they don't look ratty, and add a nice top, eyeliner, jewelry, or something snazzy. Oh, and by the way, Delta has been married to adoring and sexy Gerald MacRaney for years.

- ✔ **Set the Stage.** OK, now you understand that you can dress sexy to feel sexy, but what about when the clothes come off and there you are in your birthday suit that is very wrinkled and out of shape: Can you still feel sexy? Why not? Feel like you still need more help? Create an atmosphere that feels sexy. Use candles and soft lights, music, silk sheets, or oils (maybe not on the silk sheets). Light a fire, run a bubble bath, or put a bunch of pillows on the floor—anything that will add to the sexual experience. This will give you something else to focus on, and your partner will be so turned on by the effort and the anticipation, neither of you will be worried about your weight.

- ✔ **Try new things.** Don't be afraid to experiment. Find out about your partner's fantasy and try to figure out how to make it happen in terms you are comfortable with. Share your fantasy. You don't have to join a dominatrix cult to have an imagination. The key is to distract yourself from your own inhibitions and self-consciousness. If you titillate your brain first, the rest of your body will play along. Don't forget to Kegel!

- ✔ **Value you.** When all is said and done, you still need to believe in yourself and your worth as a human being. *God don't make no junk.* Know that the people who love you love you no matter what. Love is NOT conditional. You are just as special and wonderful as anyone else, especially to your partner. He picked you for lots of reasons and not just for the size of your tush. Besides, isn't he the guy you took care of when he had the flu, who leaves his socks on when making love, and who farts at the dinner table? He shouldn't be that hard to impress, so don't judge yourself too harshly.

I could have put a discussion on sex in several places throughout this book because it serves many physical and emotional functions. It could easily fit in with the discussion on exercise because sexual activity burns calories: Another reason to do it. The more passionate you are, the better the workout, so get busy.

Sex is also a great stress reliever. Our bodies release tension when we orgasm, so think about that too when you are feeling at the end of your rope and need to cut loose. This would be a better way to do it rather than eating, drinking, gambling, or chain smoking. Sexual contact releases endorphins, which help fight colds and flu. Not only will you feel better mentally after sex, but you will have also given your body a shot against the flu! If your partner loves you (or even if it is just recreational), sex is good for your health, just take the necessary precautions against unwanted pregnancy and sexually transmitted diseases. Use a condom!

Please also know that although I write from my own perspective, much of what I have discussed here applies to men as well as women and to same-sex partners. We all have issues with our bodies and our ability to feel sexy.

Cosmo to *Vogue*

And all of the wonderful magazines in between are great sources of inspiration. If Barbie could write, she would be an editor at a woman's magazine. These magazines are such great cheerleaders and offer pretty good tips on all kinds of issues: health, fitness, fashion, cosmetics, sex, accessories, you name it: It's in there. There is nothing better than indulging yourself with a magazine, unsweetened ice tea, and a hammock. You can learn how to dress stylishly on a budget. Delve into sexual experimentation. Read about new diet research. See new exercise moves demonstrated and get low-cal recipes. The magazines are all a bit different, so I like to vary the ones I buy. (OK, I actually read them for free on the treadmill since they are available at the gym.) When I need a fashion boost, it's *Vogue*. You can also find a lot of hilarity in some of the outfits they are hocking. When was the last time you saw someone walking down the street with a pink feathered hat, a jacket with no shirt on underneath, red velvet pants, a purse shaped like a hot dog, and leopard stilettos? (This question does not apply to readers living in Los Angeles.) These magazines can also be good for the *Laughing It Up* tip you will read about later. When I am looking for fitness motivation, I like *Shape*,

Self, or *Fitness* magazine. *Shape* and *Fitness* are great for the workout suggestions. *Health* magazine is good on food and nutrition. *Self* has a good mix of both. But mix up what you read, so you don't get bored. The magazines are also great to have on a stationary bike to keep you distracted from that little digital timer that blinks the seconds away at you. (That's why I like them at the gym, not just because they are free.)

Many other magazines specialize on certain activities, like *Runner's World* for runners or *Outdoors* for hikers. There are magazines devoted to golfing, sailing, tennis, horseback riding, kayaking, and skiing. If you want to learn more about a sport, there is a magazine about it.

Also, look for books and videos on these subjects, if you really want to learn more about a sport or to improve your skill level. They provide a more in-depth explanation than a magazine article can.

A lot of information is available on the Internet, and you can find out about clubs and associations dedicated to different sports and activities by doing a Web search.

Be a Fashion Trend Setter

Speaking of the fashion magazines, when was the last time you bought something you saw in a runway photo? If you are still wearing your sweatshirt and leggings to the mall, maybe it is time to rethink your wardrobe as well. I know I feel much better throughout my day when I have dressed the part, and fashion is an important aspect of our psyche and self-expression. The colors and style we choose say a lot about who we are and how we feel about ourselves. It is the visual image we project out to the world. Do we really want to be seen in an old T-shirt and stretch pants? Those maybe comfortable and great for cleaning the house, but do you really want to be seen in public looking like you just cleaned your house? I didn't think so.

The next few suggestions are geared to help improve your sense of wardrobe. This does not mean you have to go out and spend a fortune, but you should consider the following fashion moves to enhance your outer beauty and stroke your inner self.

- ✔ **Attack on the Black and White.** I've always heard that black makes you look thinner, which I guess it does since it absorbs light and pulls in the eye. But then one day while shopping in a trendy boutique and doing my best to pick out every black sweater they had, the 20-something sales clerk informed me that too much black would make me look old. *EH GADS!* She had me try on a dusty rose sweater, and she was right. The color picked up my complexion and I looked brighter. I've started to buy much less black, and I find that color and some prints give me a flair that inspires me throughout the day. Avoid white, however; since too much of it reflects light and makes people look bigger.

- ✔ **Monochrome it.** Still need the thinning effect you get from basic black? Try using colors such as brown and eggplant, and match the skirt, jacket and shirt. If you keep your outfit in the same color family, you will still get the elongated look you are seeking without the Old Italian mourner look you get from basic black. However, when all is said and done, the little black dress is always a wardrobe classic.

- ✔ **Prints, flowers, and stripes.** These can be dangerous, especially in larger sizes. There are tons of prints out there in today's fashion market, but you probably don't want to get too caught up in them since too much can be very unflattering and may be very out of style next season. However, they are a lot of fun and can give you an extra perk, so look for ones that will fit in with some of the wardrobe you already have and can be useful for day or evening wear. Add just a print top to a suit, but avoid dresses that are all paisley, floral, or polka dots from top to bottom. These are too distracting and take the eye all over the place, making even the thinnest among us look big. Buy trendy prints on sale since they might not make it onto next season's must-have list.

Personally, I am not big on the florals. They were cute when you were five or are good if you work in a florist, but they don't seem to have a lot of sex appeal or glamour. If you must pick the daisies, then find subtler materials, such as a cotton pastel and avoid the overdone, so no neon polyester florals, please! A few flowers strategically placed along a neckline or at the hem can help draw the eye away from your trouble spots.

Stripes are best when they are vertical since they will make you look thinner and taller (an added bonus). If the stripes are horizontal, look for patterns that are staggered. For example, horizontal stripes just across your bust on a sweater with a dark background will make those A cups look bigger, while the dark contrast narrows your waist.

✔ **The right fit.** I used to think I was fooling the world by wearing shirts that were oversized and hung down over my big butt. Now when I look at pictures from a few years ago, I realize I was fooling no one but maybe myself. If it is too big, it looks too big and you look even bigger in it, so bag the big! Buy clothes that are form fitting and complement rather than hide your curves. If a size 14 fits, wear it. Don't buy a 16 thinking it will hide your belly. The larger size will hang in the wrong places and the extra material will make you look bigger. For example, when you try on a shirt or jacket, the cuffs should come to your wrist. If they hang over, then it is probably the wrong size. Conversely, if you need a 14, don't buy the 12. If it is too tight, all of the wrong things will stick out and make you look even heavier. You may also want to try a three-quarter sleeve, which gives your arms a longer, leaner look.

✔ **Deplete the pleats.** Nothing looks worse at the waistline than pleats, especially if you have big hips. Pleats are good if you are built like a boy, but the rest of us probably don't need them. However, some great new styles have the pleats lower down, at mid-thigh, which will give you a longer look in the middle since the eye is drawn farther down the leg. So these could be an option. The classic A-line skirt is always a winner, if it is the right size.

✔ **Neck and neck.** Nothing makes me look taller and more slender than a V-neck collar, and talk about feeling sexy when I've got a hint of cleavage. An unbuttoned collared shirt is also a good alternative. If you are smaller on top, then go with a "boat" neck. It is also a sexier look, but if you are big on top, it will make you look bigger. A solid-color turtleneck with a long necklace can give you a longer, sleeker look as well. Avoid ruffles, lace, or bows at the collar unless you are small on top or in your 20s or early 30s.

✔ **A hem.** Skirts and dresses are all over when it comes to where the hemline falls. Minis are hot if you've got the gams for them, just don't go too short. No one wants to see your fanny when you bend over (well, maybe some adolescent boys do). In the winter add tights and boots for a great look. Just remember to keep them tasteful and stylish. Longer skirts are good too, and with boots are a classic. A longer casual skirt with a border at the hem can be slenderizing since it will draw the eye downward. Slits—to an appropriate height—are always sexy and slenderizing. Buttons and zippers along the slits are big these days and can add some flair and youthfulness to a look.

Pants should be cut to flatter your figure and come to the top of the heel of your shoe. Capri pants can make you look shorter and stockier if the cut is not right or you wear them with a flat shoe. Watch out for pants with big pockets on the hips and butt.

✔ **Be a heel.** I would live in my sneakers, but I like the look a shoe with a heel gives my short stubby legs. The heel doesn't have to be a spiked stiletto, but a nice shoe with even a low heel can be slenderizing to the leg. If you have a lot of walking to do, then carry the heels for when you get to the party.

Also, make sure your shoes match your outfit. If you are doing the monochrome thing, your shoes should always be darker than the rest of your outfit. Black is always a good choice, unless you are wearing a lot of pastels; then go with a basic ivory shoe. Your shoes should complement the outfit, not distract from it. Sling-backs or mules are always sexy, even in a lower heel; they're just not great in the snow. If you are short or if your feet swell, avoid straps around the ankle; they just make you look shorter and can be uncomfortable by the end of a day. And buy leather shoes. Real leather looks better, lasts longer, and won't make your feet stink! You can find real leather shoes at the same prices as the "man-made material" version if you buy them on sale or at discount stores, like Marshall's and T.J. Maxx—two of my favorite places! I've even found designer names on sale at Nordstrom's, so watch for the sales.

✔ **ACCESSORIZE.** Those little touches can add so much to an outfit. I know no matter what I am wearing, I don't feel dressed if I don't have on my earrings. A bit of jewelry can make a difference, even in a casual outfit. A long beaded chain on a monochrome outfit can really elongate your look and spice up the bland. Add a bangle, a beret, or a brooch for fun. Bangles on your wrists, especially with a three-quarter sleeve, will give your arm a longer look. Costume jewelry is making a huge comeback so enjoy the variety and inexpensive choices.

Stockings and tights can make or break a look. Stick with the classic nudes for business or match the color to the monochrome. Just be careful because if you are off, you will look silly. Personally, I don't think you need designs on your legs, unless you are trying to add a little vamp with some fishnets to a simple black dress; then go for it, honey!

A scarf can give you a hint of whimsy, which you can rely on if you don't want to wear a print blouse. Shawls can be a great alternative to an overcoat that makes you look bulky, as long as the shawl is warm enough, of course.

If you are adding hats and gloves, they should complement the scarf or shawl. Avoid too many distracting colors, which will take the eye all over the place and detract from your otherwise pulled-together look. For example, if you are wearing a scarf with an earth-tone print, then have the hat and gloves in a matching brown.

And, finally, who can forget the handbag? My mother changes hers as often as the rest of us change our underwear. She still subscribes to the theory that the bag should match the outfit. That's a lot of bags! I prefer a few basic bags that I can switch off between business and casual. Avoid the oversized bag that can carry the proverbial kitchen sink. It makes you look bigger too. Decide what you really need and take only those things with you. By doing so, you will also be doing your back and shoulders a favor. Make the bag real leather too unless you are going to the beach, then by all means carry canvas.

✔ **Hair Today.** Now that we've got you styling, let's not forget about the hair. Get a stylist to work with you and update the 'do, if you have had the same cut since college. Try some highlights and color to brighten things up. Part your hair on the side. Use scrunchies in the gym, but berets and clips for other occasions to compliment a look.

✔ **Liners, and powders, and blushes—*oh my!*** This would be makeup. Use it. Even a little liner or some mascara can open up your eyes. You don't need an hour to put on makeup. You can do it in minutes if you know your trouble zones and conquer them. Hit dark circles with concealer. Whisk on blush to heighten cheekbones. Use liner to help thin lips blossom, and open eyes with an eyelash curler and mascara. Take another few seconds and add a shade along the eye and a lighter version above it. Do the other side and you are done! Five minutes, I promise!

A Scale Note

I have heard mixed opinions about monitoring weight loss with a scale. Weight will fluctuate from day to day because of water retention; especially around the time a woman is having her period. This is not an old wives' tale! Certain foods, especially those high in salt, will also cause the body to hold fluids for a few days, so men are also subject to water weight gain, although they would never admit it. In my experience, they tend to be the ones who have the saltshaker next to them during dinner, so water weight can be a big problem for men. Because of this fluctuation, some experts say to stay away from the scale altogether, yet I like the ability to measure my successes. I have my scale near my closet and use it as my fashion consultant when I am getting dressed in the morning. (This is also the only time and place I can weigh myself when I haven't eaten in several hours and be completely naked, so I can get my "true" weight.) I get on the scale before I get dressed, and very often my weight determines the outfit. If I am feeling good about what I am wearing, the great mood that comes with it motivates me all day to make the right choices. However, if the dress fits like a circus tent, then it is even harder to feel good about myself and not want to give up. I keep thinking about the scale and don't dare have pizza for lunch! I understand that it is no big deal if from Monday to Tuesday I've gained three pounds with no trips to the buffet in between. Yet the scale helps me face the truth. Unlike well-intentioned friends who tell you how great you look, the scale won't lie, even though I have been known to check the batteries while mumbling, "This can't be right."

Keep the scale out where you can get to it easily. Someone once told me that she kept her scale near the refrigerator. She weighed herself before reaching for food. Talk about a deterrent! Figure out what's best for you. If you are working with professionals, they will weigh you, so you just might want to skip doing it yourself anyway.

You should also be checking your body mass index (BMI) against your weight as a more accurate measure of how healthy you are for your height. (See the BMI chart .) By doing this, you will be performing a check and balance for your health that will assist you in determining whether you are at your ideal weight. The BMI chart takes the guesswork out of figuring out what you should weigh. By using the chart, we do not have to rely on our own body image perception of what we should or shouldn't weigh.

Pinch Pennies and Inches

I remember years ago my Aunt Lee was trying to quit smoking. Each day she took her cigarette money and placed it in a big jar. In a few months she had saved enough money to fly from California to New York for a two-week vacation! This was a great motivator for her to stop smoking. The big money jar was a daily reminder of the goal, and the trip was a great reward for the accomplishment.

I suggest that you try this with your candy bar money. Think about how much you spend on junk food and portion it off each day in a jar. Take $2 each day or some of your spare change and put it in the biggest container you can find. Mark it with a goal: "New DVD Player." By the end of the year you will have $730 and have given yourself an added incentive not to buy junk food. This obviously works too if you are trying to quit smoking. Since cigarettes cost $4 or more a pack, you can double what you have saved. Save your smoking and junk food money and you will have $2,190 to do something special. That's incentive!

Getting Beyond the Plateau

Everyone who has ever dieted before knows what I mean by "the plateau." It happens when you have been on a real roll. You have lost the recommended one to two pounds a week over the last six months, but now several weeks have passed and you can't get the needle on the scale to move one smidgeon. "What am I doing wrong?" you wonder. You check your personal fitness plan and food log and can't find any indiscretions to blame. You feel frustrated and disgusted. All of this work for *nothing*! You make a mental note to be mad at your mother and her genetics when she asks you how your diet is going.

Take a deep breath, because the plateau syndrome is not imaginary. Your body has adjusted to your new weight and your metabolism has slowed again to conserve the energy your body thinks it needs. This is the time when you are most at risk for quitting. It is easier to keep up with a healthy living lifestyle when you can see the success and buy new clothes, but weight management is just not as interesting. If you truly feel good about your diet, do not put pressure on yourself to eat less. Doing so will just add to your sense of frustration and cause you to eat more. You may feel frustrated and challenged to stay motivated when you are at the plateau point. But fear not! Here are the tips for handling the plateau.

- ✔ Call your mother and blame her. (Just kidding.) If she is a support person for you, call her or anyone else who has really cheered you on and let them know about your frustrations. Sometimes venting is all you need to do. Call a friend and add an activity to your weekend.

- ✔ Contact your dietitian or primary care provider and ask for advice and recommendations. It may be time to go back in and reevaluate your plan.

- ✔ Reevaluate your fitness plan on your own before thinking about cutting any more calories. Can you add five minutes or increase resistance during your cardio workout? Are you doing strength training? Remember, muscle burns more calories than fat, so add or increase weights/resistance when you work out. Building muscle is key to weight loss and can be the best way to beat the plateau phenomenon.

- ✔ Go shopping! Since this is my solution for a lot of things anyway, why not now too? The first time you bought a size 10 instead of a 14 felt pretty darn good, so why not relive that experience and reaffirm how much you have already accomplished? You don't have to buy everything you try on, but try, try, try! You may also want to buy yourself that new CD you have wanted and listen to it when you increase your workout.

- ✔ Keep your nose to the grindstone and drive on. This is about a lifestyle, remember, not a diet. Keep with it. If you are still not at your goal weight or BMI, recognize that eventually you will be. Practice the positive visualizations and affirmations outlined in the *Stress Management* tips section.

STRESS MANAGEMENT TIPS

Stress. Everybody's got it. Work. School. Family. Friends. Deadlines. Commitments. Obligations. Checkbooks. Laundry. Soccer practice. Bad hair. How do we handle stress? Well, you know the answer to this one: We eat, and usually the wrong things. We are using food to help us deal with our emotions whether we realize it or not. We seek out "comfort foods," like pizza and chocolate cake, which are high-fat items, but are actually broken down more slowly by the body when we are under stress. Unfortunately, that makes us feel worse, tired, and ready to give up. I once read that stress is caused by the inability to choke someone who desperately needs it, but actually stress is caused by feeling out of control and overwhelmed. As I said earlier, weight loss is really about healthy living, not quick-fix diets and flashy exercise equipment. So it is important to think not just about diet and exercise, but about overall healthy habits and how to feel better about yourself and your life, which you do have control over. This sense of control will extend to your emotional well-being and mental health too.

Stress is often one of the hardest things for our bodies to overcome. It weakens our immune system, leaves us tired, causes headaches and stomachaches, and leads to depression and defeatist behavior. We are less likely to think rationally when we are under duress and are less likely to make the right choices for ourselves, much less make a commitment to do something soothing. Although that is just what we do need, we are too stressed to see it.

I believe that the conundrum of this century is that with all of our convenience items—cell phones, e-mail, Palm Pilots, faxes, and microwaves — we live in a world that just might be too fast-paced for our emotional stability. Were we really created to do all the things and interact with all of the people that we do in one day? We are doing more with less and are working smarter, but our environment is more stressful than ever before and we are getting fatter to boot. Perhaps we have created a society that our minds and spirits cannot cope with sufficiently, which maybe why stress-related diseases and disorders (i.e., tension headaches, panic attacks, heart attacks, etc.) are on the rise.

If you think you might have more complicated emotional issues or have been diagnosed with *posttraumatic stress disorder (PTSD)* or *depression,* which are more common diagnoses among women than men, you should seek professional mental health counseling. If you have been a victim of abuse, rape, crime, disaster, an accident, or some other type of tragic event, you may suffer from symptoms that your coping mechanisms cannot handle. You may be overeating, abusing alcohol or drugs, overworking, or engaging in risky behaviors to escape from the memories and bad feelings that are upsetting to you. A trained mental health professional can help you sort out these feelings and find healthier coping strategies. Some of the tips outlined in this section may help, but it is important to deal with the more complex underlying emotional issues and purge distressing memories and self-loathing thoughts. Doing that may take professional help. It is also possible that you are going through a temporary difficult time (bereavement, job loss) and just need help dealing with your grief. Counseling is not a sign of weakness and it does not mean you are crazy, unless you've got a hat made of tinfoil; then I'd wonder—or maybe you were just reading *Vogue.*

Know the signs and symptoms of more serious mental health issues by looking at the next chart. If you answer yes to two or more of these symptoms in either category, you may want to consider discussing this with your primary care provider, especially if you have experienced a traumatic event, are drinking or abusing drugs (or other risky behavior), have contemplated suicide, or if family and friends have told you they are worried about you.

Mental Health Problem Signs and Symptoms	
Posttraumatic Stress Disorder	**Depression**
Experienced or witnessed a traumatic event	Constantly feeling sad or empty
Nightmares	Lack of interest in social activities, sex, or hobbies
Intrusive thoughts	Changes in appetite and weight gain or loss
Difficulty falling or staying asleep	Difficulty in falling or staying asleep
Guilt for surviving	Restless, fatigued, tired
Anxiety and/or depression	Indecisive and distracted
Anger and rage	Feeling worthless or guilty
Hopeless about future	Feeling suicidal

The following exercises and tips are some of my thoughts on how to combat daily stress and other bad-hair-day events. We sometimes don't even realize that we are under stress. It just builds up gradually over time. Begin by identifying your stressors and then use the tips to help reduce the effects stress is having on your life and your eating habits.

Inventory Your Stress

To help get a handle on your stress, think about what causes it. Each of us will find different situations stressful or not. What may stress you out may not even bother your sister or best friend. We each have our own stress levels and tolerances.

The first step in dealing with stress is to be able to recognize the warning signs before you are shrieking and screeching uncontrollably at the TV remote. How do you know when you are feeling stressed out? How does your body react to stress? How bad is it? How are you coping with it?

Use the chart to help you identify what your stressors are and how well you are coping. Make a few blank copies of the chart so you can use it over time. List the things that are stressful to you and rate them on a scale of 1 (low) to 10 (high). What emotions do you feel when you think about your ex-husband, family finances, or the recent death of your father? How are you coping with those emotions? Could you be handling a situation in a better way? Is there someone you can call for support: family, clergy, or a therapist? Is there a peer support program at your local community center or hospital? Have you tried long walks and hot baths? What about prayer, meditation, or yoga? Take a moment and brainstorm your own ideas to improve your coping skills.

Use you new coping strategy techniques for a few days or a week. Then chart your stress again. Has your stress rating score gone down? Are your emotions less intense? If your new coping technique is working, your stress level should go down over time. It may be gradual or even fluctuate. Keep working at this until you can get your stress level to a 1 or 2. If your stress level is not going down with ideas you have tried on your own, you should seek professional or peer support for a more focused approach to stress reduction. You may need to consult with a physician to discuss medication options, especially if you are experiencing other physical symptoms, such as migraines or high blood pressure. Share this chart with your primary care provider, so he or she can see what you have been doing to manage your stress.

CHART YOUR STRESS				
Stressor	**Rate stress (scale 1–10)**	**Emotions**	**Coping Strategy**	**New Coping Strategy**
Example: Divorce	8	Angry and frustrated	Yelling at kids, eating late at night	Call a peer support friend and get out

Positive People/Positive Time Plan

If you started reading this book from the beginning, then you probably have already thought about your life's story. You have taken the time to think and write about your past and your future goals, but how do you feel about your present? If your dreams are on hold, ask yourself: Why? Think about the things you want to accomplish, such as going back to school or on a vacation, then put them on the *Positive Planner* and set a date to do them.

Go back and look at your Positive Forces and Energy Zappers list. Are there more positive people in your life than those who make you feel burdened? Are you doing the things you want to do? If not, make an effort to spend more time with the people you enjoy and zap the zappers.

You could:

- ✔ Invite a positive force friend to join you on a walk or go for a hike.
- ✔ Make an appointment with someone for your very own play date and add it to your planner.
- ✔ Start your own Guacamole Club or join Overeaters Anonymous, a 12-step support program that holds regular meetings. You can find information on the Web at *www.overeatersanonymous.org*.
- ✔ Take the kids on a nature hike. Remember that if you have a weight problem, your kids are likely to have your genes and your habits. Get them in shape as well.
- ✔ Walk the dog. Your best friend needs the exercise too. Fido can be a real motivator since he is always so happy when you spend time with him.
- ✔ Make friends with people at the gym (if you join); they are likely to have the same mind-set about healthy habits as you have. They will also know some good tips and which classes to take.

- ✔ Make unsweetened iced tea and read a book outdoors on a sunny day.
- ✔ Sneak off to an afternoon movie.
- ✔ Sign up and train for a 5K run.
- ✔ Visit an art gallery.
- ✔ Learn how to crochet.
- ✔ Take a golfing lesson with your partner or a friend (pick any sport, dance, or art)
- ✔ Shop!
- ✔ Fly a kite.
- ✔ Get out a hula-hoop and twist again!
- ✔ Call someone you miss and say, "Hi."
- ✔ Write a real letter; OK, e-mail it
- ✔ Join an online "Diet Pals" website (see *www.webMD.com*).
- ✔ Write *Your Story* as described earlier in this book.

What are some things you can do or have always wanted to do, but have not made the time to do recently? (List them on the chart on the following page.)

Now go back to each item you listed and write down a plan or a date to get it accomplished. How will you make your activity happen? Whom will you involve? Check your *Positive People* list and invite one or two of them to join in. Having something to look forward to can be a real motivator!

POSITIVE PLANNER	
To Do	**Completion Plan**
Example: Sign up for The Race for the Cure	Train for 5 weeks and finish race in ½ hour. Get Amy to sign up too.

Laugh It Up

Have you not yet heard that laughter is the best medicine, especially for stress? The endorphins you release during hysterical laughter can give you the same euphoric feeling as a runner's high and are known to also reduce pain. Laughter stimulates the neurological and cardiovascular systems, burns calories, and helps fight stress and depression. As adults, we have gotten so serious that we have forgotten how to laugh. Researchers have found that children laugh up to 400 times a day, but adults laugh only about 15 times a day. Talk about being uptight!

I once worked with a cancer patient who had his wife bring him in videos of the TV sitcom *Murphy Brown* because he felt getting a good laugh reduced his pain and helped him sleep better. Norman Cousins wrote about this phenomenon in his landmark book, *Anatomy of an Illness,* when he was sick in the 1960s. He used laughter to help reduce his pain from ankylosing spondylitis.

So, on the cold rainy days when you want to keep the sneakers in the closet, rent an old Marx Brothers movie, invite friends over, pop low-fat popcorn, and laugh it up. Some *Duck Soup* may be just what you need to lower your stress level.

A good joke or a smile is the best tension reliever. It is hard to be mad at someone when you are smiling at *him.* (*He* is usually the one giving you a tension headache, isn't he?) Whenever you are feeling stressed and find yourself needing to count to 10, don't just count; embellish by imagining the situation with camels spitting in the background or all your coworkers being pushed into a tiny car by clowns and driven away. Your imagination is probably better than mine, so think of the most ridiculous thing you can and add it to the mix. (See more about this under *Meditations, Visualizations and Other Great Fantasies* tip.) Once you find yourself smiling at your own silliness, go back to solving the problem. You will be calmer and better able to think it through without feeling overwhelmed and ready for a trip to the kitchen or the snack bar.

Add these things to your day for a smile break:

- ✔ Keep toys on your desk for a quick fix break.
- ✔ Listen to the funniest DJ you can find on the radio for your morning commute.
- ✔ Memorize a joke each day and tell it to someone else. (Just keep it politically correct!)
- ✔ Rent a George Carlin video (my all-time favorite comedian).
- ✔ Watch a TV sitcom.
- ✔ Read the funnies first in the newspaper.
- ✔ Laugh with your kids—they are the experts, after all.
- ✔ Actually wear the sweater your mother-in-law gave you last Christmas.

Beauty Rest

Do you get enough sleep?

❑ Yes ❑ No

The average adult needs eight hours of sleep per night, which studies have shown helps control hormone secretion and metabolism. I guess that's why they call it beauty rest. I know that when I have not slept well, not only am I ready to strangle the people who annoy me, but I also feel sluggish and unmotivated for most of the day. And you know what that means: Sugar! You are overworked, underpaid, and don't have the time to do all of the things on your to-do list. What do you do when the kids are up sick, your unfinished Sprocket Sales Improvement Report is due early the next morning, and your husband is in the mood? Try this:

- ✔ **Plan better and make your plans known.** Organizing, prioritizing, and communicating your needs to get done all of the tasks that need to be accomplished during the day will help you sleep better at night. We often forget to ask for help; do it, don't be a martyr, and get a good night's sleep.

- ✔ **Set a sleep routine.** Don't stay up late watching the *Late Show* just because it is the weekend. Go to sleep at the same time every night and get up at the same time each morning.

- ✔ **Quit caffeine.** If you are counting coffee cups and not sheep, it is a sign that you are overindulging in caffeine during the day. Switch to decaffeinated coffee or tea and get caffeine-free soda. Also avoid other stimulants, such as nicotine and alcohol, in the evening, if you use them at all.

- ✔ **Make the atmosphere in your bedroom soothing.** Don't clutter your nightstand with books, papers, and reports that need to be read. You will be tempted to eye them all night. Keep the room at a comfortable temperature and dark when you are sleeping.

- ✔ **Exercise during the day.** A good workout *earlier* in the day will help you feel more relaxed since you will have burned energy. When you work out too late at night, you are releasing too much adrenaline to be able to fall asleep.

- ✔ **Get fresh air.** Taking your workout outdoors is especially helpful in improving sleep.

- ✔ **Relax with yoga or meditation.** Get comfy and unwind before going to bed. The following pages contain more tips on yoga and relaxation that you can try at night.

- ✔ **Hot tub it.** There is nothing like a good old-fashioned bubble bath to make you feel pampered and relaxed. Add a candle and a glass of wine. Place cucumbers on your eyes and a mudpack on your face, and bye-bye, world.

- ✔ **The in-the-mood husband might just have the right idea.** There is no better stress reliever than sex. So take the 10 minutes he needs and then be snoring the night away.

- ✔ **Seek medical advice.** If you are having difficulty sleeping because of nightmares or other intrusive thoughts, you may want to contact your primary care provider and discuss counseling or medication as an option.

Hatha, Anusara, Sivananda, and Pilates

These are forms of yoga (not Yoda; that was the little guy in *Star Wars*) and other stretching exercises. I could have stuck more about yoga and Pilates in the exercise section, since they are great flexibility workouts and my muscles feel it afterward, but I find them to be more relaxing than anything else. Since yoga movements are done in conjunction with breath inhalations and exhalations, I find it has also helped to improve my breathing.

The practice of yoga was first described over 5,000 years ago in India as a joining of mind and body. Yoga is a series of more than 200 poses or stretching positions done in symmetry to one's breath. Many forms of yoga are done all over the world. I've seen Korean yoga being practiced in a park; it is very different from the Hatha yoga I first learned at a class in the gym. Pilates is a method of body-sculpting exercises created by Joseph Pilates in the 1920s that involves fewer, more precise movements requiring control and form.

I can't tell you all that much about the many different types of yoga, mostly because I really don't care to find out. It isn't my goal to become the flower child of this decade, but to tone and stretch my body and relax my mind, which are the Hindu principles of yoga. In one of my first yoga classes, I got so relaxed that I began to snore! If you are worried about looking or sounding foolish in a yoga class trying to contort into all those strange positions, don't worry; I have already taken care of that, so you can go and feel free to enjoy it!

Yoga is based on a series of moves, called asanas. You can do these hundreds of poses and postures (i.e., down dog, mountain, warrior, lotus, plank, cobra, bridge, etc.) at your own skill level to flex and stretch individually targeted muscles. The different asanas improve your flexibility and strength, add to endurance, improve posture and breathing, and reduce stress and tension stored in the body. If you do want to learn more about yoga, take a class, buy another book or video, or look online (see *Internet Resources*) for the centers (ashrams) near you that teach yoga and/or Pilates. Most fitness centers offer various types of yoga or Pilates as part of their class schedules. If you are thinking about joining a gym, find out if they offer such classes. If you don't want to join an expensive gym to take an occasional yoga class, try your local community centers, hospitals, or private instructors who will give classes from their homes for far less than the cost of joining a gym.

The two most important things I can share with you about yoga and Pilates is not to have burritos for lunch beforehand and to wear panties. I have heard my share of flatulence as the result of the pose of a child and have seen enough pubic hair during down dog to know these are two very important tips. Since hyena laughing is not a yoga position, it would help the rest of us maintain our composure during these intense and delicate moves if everyone would comply with eating right before yoga and wearing the proper attire. Ooo-Mmm.

Meditations, Visualizations, and Other Great Fantasies

Using simple meditations and visualizations can be a quick way to interrupt stressful thoughts and reactions during your day, especially if you have intrusive thoughts or bad memories that keep you from concentrating and send you running to the fridge for comfort. I am more prone to want to spent my time clearing my mind of daily stress by fantasizing about a deserted island and David Duchovny, but with my luck, his wife, Téa Leoni, would show up with a bunch of crazed prehistoric dinosaurs and we would all have to race through the jungle to avoid being trampled to death. Maybe that is why I should not be left alone to visualize. But meditation and visualization can be very helpful relaxation techniques to ease your mind when the tension builds.

In order to meditate, you can lie down or sit back with your spine straight in a chair, close your eyes, and, while breathing deeply in and out, relax your body. Keep your mind clear and just concentrate on the sensations in your body as you focus on each area. When exhaling, mentally release the tension in each muscle and organ and say to yourself,

"My feet are relaxed.

My legs are relaxed.

My pelvis is relaxed.

My abdomen is relaxed.

My chest is relaxed.

My neck is relaxed.

My shoulders are relaxed.

My arms are relaxed.

My head is relaxed."

Visualizations can also be a very helpful way of reducing stress. You may need to take a break by lying down or sitting back more comfortably in a chair, closing your eyes, and creating an image of a harmonious scene in your mind. If the beach is your ideal place, then see it as all yours (no tourists with oversized umbrellas and boom boxes or cancer-causing rays). Add the sound of a breeze and the smell of the ocean. Taste the salt in the air. Feel the warmth of the *non–cancer-causing* sun and the mist from the *non-polluted* waves spray over your body. Run your toes through the sand. Now tell yourself that things are OK and you can handle it. Stay positive and affirming about yourself and free yourself from your stress.

You can also use visualization to achieve your goals, whether they include losing weight, finding a soul mate, or getting a promotion. See every aspect of the desired outcome. Think about all of the new clothes, the great guy, or the plush corner office. Enjoy and savor your success. Then search your heart and soul for your hidden fears and lack of confidence in yourself. Identify the ways in which you have sabotaged yourself in the past when you have tried to reach new goals. How have you behaved? What has held you back? Focus in on those fears and inabilities. Tell yourself these are irrational beliefs. Even if they were true once, that does not make them true forever. Begin to refute these irrational fears by compartmentalizing each one and picking it apart. If you have had bad experiences, realize they were not awful. Think of the things you did learn and how you coped. You have survived them and have learned and grown. Go back to your original vision of success and think through the steps it would take to reach your desired goals. You can turn this into more of an active exercise by using your journal. Log your desired goal; write down the date, what your fears and obstacles are, and what the solutions would be. You can also use the Visualization Log . Write out your action plan. When you have completed one of the tasks, go back and date it. Repeat the visualization each time you work on achieving your goal. Recite the *Attitude Is Everything* affirmations.

As noted earlier, you can use humor in your visualizations and try to make yourself laugh. Your real-life stress (i.e., your boss) can't be worse than running for your life from deranged dinosaurs with Téa and David on a deserted island. Your boss may make you nervous, but he won't think of you as dinner, unless you are a lion tamer, maybe. I like adding humor to situations and making them seem more ridiculous than they actually are. If *Tyrannosaurus rex* crashed your conference, that wouldn't be as bad or as awful as the air conditioning being on the fritz at the sumo wrestlers' convention you have planned. Sweating sumos (although unpleasant) is not as awful as having them become sumo-soufflés for dinosaurs. Humor helps us realize that although a situation maybe bad or tragic, it is not overwhelmingly awful. We can find a way to handle it without having to run to the candy counter. We are less likely to overeat because of the stress if we minimize it before it builds up. Now, that is dinosaur slaying, Mr. Spielberg!

VISUALIZATION LOG
Date:
What is your desired goal?
Fears or obstacles: ✔ ✔ ✔
What makes these fears irrational? (Is there any humor?) ✔ ✔ ✔
What would be the solution? ✔ ✔ ✔
Plan of action: ✔ ✔ ✔
Date completed: ✔ ✔ ✔

Religion, Rituals, and Rites

For most of us, religion or spirituality offers meaning and a sense of order in our lives. It gives us strength, purpose, and hope for the future. It is how we know we are loved and worthy. It is a source of great solace when we are faced with a crisis, trauma, or difficult decision. We turn to our belief in God, goddesses, or some other sense of a higher power when we need to feel protected and loved. Regardless of our religious affiliation, spirituality gives most of us a sense of comfort, guidance, and peace. It contributes to our state of equilibrium and balance as human beings when we let God lead. It is how we connect to our own heritage and the community around us, even if we describe ourselves as secular or atheists.

Yet we sometimes take all of this for granted and neglect our spiritual well-being as we rush through our busy days, even when we are trying to make an attempt to nurture our minds and bodies. Reading psalms or daily meditations, engaging in morning prayer or holiday observances is important in giving us something to hold on to, especially when we are struggling with difficult questions about life or are trying to cope with a stressful situation (or even when we are trying to improve our health and lose weight).

Prayer, worship, or meditation helps us find fulfillment and acts to reduce stress when we are faced with problems, dilemmas, and crises. The rituals associated with religious practices give us the symbolic gestures that offer strength, hope, and faith for the future. We need these things to face the daily stresses (big and small) and the demands placed on our lives by the things we cannot control. Rituals connect us to our ancestors who have gone before us and help us to realize that there are things that transcend time and circumstance. With a little faith, we too can find our path. Sometimes we need to remember that God gives us what we need, but not necessarily what we want.

A great deal of support can be found in being part of a congregation. Members of the same religious community can offer each other friendship, guidance, assistance, and information. Most religious institutions offer to the community at large (not just their members) programs that are not only spiritual, but also educational and enjoyable. These programs are also great opportunities for volunteerism and to give back to your community. Some of these programs are geared for different age groups. There are also programs for singles and others for families with children. Look in local newspapers and circulars for services or events that might interest you.

We know how to feed our bodies and sometimes we may even remember to feed our minds, but our spiritual side needs to be tended to as well, if we are to feel balanced and centered. When we are spiritually at peace, pure of heart, and living in the light, then we take better care of ourselves overall, which improves our health and functioning.

Self-Talk: a.k.a. Talking to Yourself

When I was a kid, I can remember my dad in the backyard talking to himself with only the trees around when he was upset about something or other. (Usually, at these times, he was wearing an old bathrobe, black socks, and smoking a cigar.) The good news is that he rarely took out his troubles by yelling at me, which somewhat made up for the embarrassment of thinking that the neighbors would see him in the yard. There was a time when the mental health professionals might have only seen psychosis in this sort of behavior, but today more and more psychiatrists and psychologists recommend this technique to their patients as a means of defusing a stressful situation. Talking to yourself no longer means you're crazy, it just means you recognize good company when you see it! If people ask, "Who you are talking to," proudly say, "Myself" and act surprised that they don't ever do it.

So, when the boss has just dumped a new project on your desk, which means you will have to work all weekend, or your child has just broken the vase Great Aunt Edna gave you and she will be there in an hour, calm yourself down by verbally telling yourself to "calm down" and "not to worry" and by using the meditation and visualization techniques you've learned. Tell yourself that the situation is not worth getting all worked up over and find the ridiculousness in the situation. Use your sense of humor as described in the *Meditation and Visualization* tips *and Attitude*

Is Everything affirmations. Take deep cleansing breaths and let go of your tension. Remind yourself of all of the good things you have going on in your life, and keep the current situation in perspective. Assure yourself that you can handle it and that you will find a way to make it work.

Self-talk will help you take the time you need to not feel overwhelmed, which leads to stress buildup and overeating, and to find positive ways of coping and problem solving: you just might not want to do it in your bathrobe with a cigar.

Massage Message

I can't think of anything more relaxing than treating myself to a massage; even one of those 10-minute jobs in a chair is a treat. I have seen masseuses in airports with chairs offering passengers an opportunity to get a massage before boarding a long flight. I think this is a great idea, especially with tensions higher during air travel these days.

When my Guacamole Club went to the Coolfont Resort in the hills of West Virginia, it was the best vacation I'd had in a long time. We got facials and massages, and my body felt rejuvenated and refreshed. It was the ultimate treat, an indulgence I would recommend to anyone, especially if you bring along your friends to engage in all of the other stress-reducing activities that come with having a pack of women all in one room.

Massage helps to alleviate tension because the deep pressure stimulates the nerves and reduces the hormones (cortisol and epinephrine) that are key in kicking us into a stress mode. These are the hormones that are activated when we are faced with a "fight, fright, or flight" scenario. This was very useful to our cavewoman ancestors, who were actually being chased by Jurassic mammoths, but is not so helpful now when it's a puppy that has just peed on the rug. Massage also releases brain chemicals that help elevate our mood. Giving a message to someone else can also make you feel more relaxed and less anxious.

Not sure about a professional massage? Here are some things to consider:

- ✔ Training, licensure, and certification of the facility and the masseuse.
- ✔ Length of massage for the price.
- ✔ Your ability to tell the therapist about your problem areas and what you want worked on most.
- ✔ Type of massage: there are different techniques, such as Swedish or Shiatsu.
- ✔ Modesty concerns. Yes, you are naked, but there is always a sheet and you can ask to have certain parts of your body touched or not touched. If you are still uncomfortable, then keep on your underwear. Let the person know if it is your first massage and have her explain things to you.
- ✔ Talk about your expectations before making the appointment, and then reiterate them with the therapist to make sure your concerns have been transmitted.

You may also want to learn some simple message techniques on your own that you and your partner can share, which can improve your level of intimacy and comfort with each other. I have learned some self-massage techniques in my yoga class that help relax my face, neck, shoulders, and head; that's another plus for learning more about yoga. There are books that teach massage techniques, and you can purchase your own massage oils and aromatherapy candles.

Get Some Sun

About 10 years ago, I traveled to Reykjavik, Iceland, during the spring and their season of "White Nights," a time of year when the sun hardly goes down. That seemed great to me. It was midnight and it was just getting dusk. However, a local woman told me the downside to the sun being up all of the time: during the other half of the year, the sun is down and it is dark most of the day. This led to a great problem for many people, who were depressed, listless, and unmotivated for that part of the year. Since then I have seen studies on seasonal affective disorder (SAD) that document the effects of the lack of sunlight on the human psyche. It seems that the lack of sunlight results in the lack of Vitamin D and hormone production in our systems and slows the flow of blood to our brains, which, in turn, can affect our mood. Additional sunlight can improve mood, increase metabolism to burn more calories, and suppresses appetite.

If you think about it: How much time do you spend outdoors during your average workweek? You go from the house, to the car, to the office, back into the car, dry cleaner, bank, take-out place, and back to the house. If you add up all of your "duck-ins" and "duck-outs," you probably spend 15 minutes in the fresh air. In the summer, you convince yourself that it's too hot to be without air conditioning; in the winter, it's just too cold to be out there. Remember how mom always wanted you outside to get some fresh air? It might have helped her keep the house clean to get rid of you for a few hours, but she was on to something. Going out to play is good for your health. The older we get, the less time we spend outdoors, which affects our health, mood, and aging. We need to get back to our sun-worshiping youth. We just need to make sure we use sunscreen on the beach and not Crisco.

You can boost your energy level and feel less stressed by getting outdoors. It will also help you get a better night's sleep. This is another good reason to walk places or put on sneakers at lunchtime. To reap the benefits of the sun, you can also sit near a window and keep the blinds open at work. Look for window seats on the bus or train. Use bright artificial light in your office or at home. And, if you can, head to Cancún in February for a sun fix!

Stinky Stuff

Candles, salts, soaks, scrubs, bubbles, beads, lotions, and masks are all wonderful ways to take care of your mind and body at the same time. When you pamper your body, your mind also reaps the benefits. The products that are meant to care for your skin, hair, and toenails also allow you the time to spend relaxing. When you've got apricot-banana goop in your hair and cucumber mud on your face—and, I hope, no one nearby for miles—you have found the solitude you need to de-stress your life. Take a few minutes to soak in a bubble bath or give yourself a facial. Light a candle and listen to music while making dinner.

Manicures and pedicures are not only a great way to pamper yourself, they are also important for healthy fingers and toes. Keeping your nails clipped and cleaned helps avoid infection and reduces bacteria. Get your cuticles cut or do it yourself. Find a fabulous polish that works with your skin tone or just a clear coat to keep nails strong.

Now, I know some of these products can be more expensive than others, but look for sales, use gift certificates, or just treat yourself! The Body Shop and Bath and Body Works have some great items that are not too expensive, especially when they run sales. I personally like anything with eucalyptus from Bath and Body Works and the foot scrub from the Body Shop. If you don't mind a bit more high-end, try any of the facial products available at Sephora's that are good for your skin type. Origins has some good scrubs and facial products too. Find what works for you and add the ones I like to your Holiday gift-shopping list. By adding these simple things to your life and letting yourself enjoy their fresh scents and rejuvenating qualities, you are actually improving your overall health.

A FINAL NOTE FOR EVERYDAY

IF YOU HAVE GOTTEN anything at all out of reading this book, it should be that taking care of yourself goes beyond a crash diet. Maintaining a healthy body weight is just one component of healthy living, which is better achieved through a body, mind, and spirit connection. When you have this balance in your life, you will feel better and live better.

You must ensure that your emotional, mental, and spiritual needs are being met just as your physical ones are. You must take care of your body with proper nutrition and hydration, exercise (cardio, strength, and flexibility training), pampering, and rest. Emotionally, you need to laugh, play, have sex, and dance with people who are supportive and inspiring. You need to mentally challenge yourself with ideas and projects that help you learn and grow, so you can be proud of yourself and your accomplishments. Regardless of your faith, you need to find a sense of purpose and meaning for your life that gives you strength and hope to face the obstacles and hurts that life will throw your way. If you make these goals your daily priority, then you will be living a healthier lifestyle.

Don't just read this book and put it back on the shelf. Make sure to complete the sections where you are to fill in the blanks. Take the time and do this for yourself, so you know what you need and where to begin. Make that doctor's appointment and take the checklist with you. Flag the tips that apply to you the most. Cut them out and paste them up where you can see them if you need the reminders right in front of you. Check out the other resources on the websites listed on the following pages.

Find the people, places, and things that motivate you and inspire you to do the right things for yourself. Get rid of the junk, and not just the junk food. Reduce the number of the people in your life who drag you down and burn you out. Live your life to its fullest. Set your goals and take the steps you need to achieve them. Don't wait to be happy. Life is too short to bargain-shop with yourself. Know that many other women and men are battling the same struggles and that you are not alone. The support is out there. With the right tools and materials, you can do anything. I know because if I can, you can too.

Quick Reference List
Review of Things to Do

If you like shopping lists, this is for you!

- ✔ Make an appointment with your primary care provider to discuss your weight and get a physical exam.
- ✔ Get free stuff on healthy living and disease management from your primary care provider, clinic, or library.
- ✔ Buy new sneakers.
- ✔ Ladies: you do need a sports bra.
- ✔ Buy new clothes. Get spandex, if you must!
- ✔ Try a new makeup and a new hairstyle.
- ✔ Try tofu and soy milk at least one time.
- ✔ Read *Shape* magazine (my favorite) but go with *Cosmo* if that is more you.
- ✔ Get a workout buddy (this is free).
- ✔ Try a workout video or DVD—your library may lend these.
- ✔ Incorporate cardio, strength, and flexibility training into your routine.

- ✔ Kegel.
- ✔ Buy a low-fat/low-calorie cookbook—they've usually got great tofu recipes!
- ✔ Light a candle while you cook dinner.
- ✔ Schedule a massage or at least get your nails done.
- ✔ Use a refreshing lotion after the shower.
- ✔ Journal your own story and tips.
- ✔ Complete the fill-in-the-blank exercises in this book.
- ✔ Surf the Web for more tips and information. (Drug Company websites are full of new research information and are credible. Be careful with some sites. Not everything on the Web is from a credible source. The most credible sites end in .gov, .edu., or .org. As a general rule, .coms are usually commercial sites that are selling their products. This does not mean that they are bad; just beware. As with any other purchase, shop and compare value.) See the *Internet Resources* listed on the following pages for credible information.

Healthy Living Activities
Daily Reminder Checklist

Clip this checklist and keep it handy as a reminder to engage in all of the healthy living tips and techniques discussed in this book.

Today I:

- ❑ Took my medication
- ❑ Took my multivitamins and minerals
- ❑ Drank 8 glasses of water
- ❑ Limited my fat calories
- ❑ Limited my carbohydrate calories
- ❑ Ate antioxidants
- ❑ Ate fiber
- ❑ Exercised:
    - ❑ Cardio
    - ❑ Strength
    - ❑ Flexibility
- ❑ Relaxed
- ❑ Laughed

Internet Resources

Cancer

- ✔ *www.AICR.org* – American Institute for Cancer Research has information on obesity and cancer.
- ✔ *www.Koman.org* – Susan G. Komen Foundation provides information on breast cancer and self-examinations.
- ✔ *www.tcrc.acor.org* – The Testicular Cancer Resource Center provides information on the disease and how to conduct self-examinations.

Children

- ✔ *www.pe4life.com* – Supports advancements in physical education programs for children.
- ✔ *www.pecentral.org* – Physical education materials for teachers, parents and students.
- ✔ *www.aahperd.org* – Joins together six national organizations that support health, physical education, recreation and dance.
- ✔ *www.espnplayyourway.com* – An initiative from Team ESPN and DisneyHand to enable kids to be active by making up games.

Diabetes

- ✔ *www.diabetes.org* – The American Diabetes Association has materials on diabetes management.

Exercise and Fitness

- ✔ *www.acsm.org* – The American College of Sports Medicine offers exercise and weight training tips.
- ✔ *www.aaai-ismafitness.com* – The American Aerobic Association/International Sports Medicine Association.
- ✔ *www.americaonthemove.org* – America on the Move is an initiative to get people more physically active.
- ✔ *www.nata.org* – The National Athletic Trainers' Association can help you find Certified Athletic Trainers.
- ✔ *www.ace.org* – The American Council on Exercise can help you locate a personal trainer near you.
- ✔ *www.nasm.org* – The National Academy of Sports Medicine can help you locate a personal trainer near you.
- ✔ *www.HealthClubs.com* – This can help you find a health club near you.
- ✔ *www.ihrsa.org* – The International Health, Racquet, and Sportsclub Association offers health club information.
- ✔ *www.curvesinternational.com* – This site helps you find a Curves near you.
- ✔ *www.pilates-studio.com* – This site explains the Joseph Pilates method.

- ✔ *www.presidentschallenge.org* – An interactive site that promotes physical activity for all ages.

- ✔ *www.yogasite.com* – This site offers yoga techniques and resources.

- ✔ *www.yogadirectory.com* – This directory helps you find a yoga center and other resources online or near you.

- ✔ *www.americanrunning.org* – Provides guidance on fitness and competitive running. Has a great guide on how to buy sneakers!

Health and Nutrition

- ✔ *www.webMD.com* – Everything you can imagine about health and fitness can be found here! You can also find a Diet Buddy on this site. Register for an online newsletter.

- ✔ *www.EatRight.org* – This is the official site of the American Dietetic Association. It offers information on nutrition and a Registered Dietitian locator by zip code.

- ✔ *www.fda.gov* – This government site offers general health information.

- ✔ *www.mypyramid.gov* – This government site offers details of the new food pyramid and tools for using it.

- ✔ *www.nal.usda.gov/fnic/foodcomp* – You can find the USDA Nutrient Database here.

- ✔ *www.4woman.gov* – This government site provides general information on women's health issues.

- ✔ *www.Health.nih.gov* – This government site offers medical and health information as well as research studies on various diseases and treatments.

- ✔ *www.weightwatchers.com* – Weight Watchers offers healthy recipes and a weight- loss program.
- ✔ *www.Jennycraig.com* – This site offers healthy recipes and a weight-loss program.
- ✔ *www.atkinscenter.com* – This site offers information on the Atkins diet.
- ✔ *www.ediet.com* – Here you can find healthy recipes and an electronic newsletter.
- ✔ *www.nutrio.com* – Help with diet and fitness is offered at this site.
- ✔ *www.fit.com* – This site also provides help with diet and fitness.
- ✔ *www.Oprah.com* – This website provides all kinds of healthy living stuff and steamy relationship tips for the added inspiration.
- ✔ *www.MayoClinic.com* – The Mayo Clinic offers health information on a wide variety of diseases and treatments.
- ✔ *www.Healthwise.org* – This site provides self-care guides and handbooks on health-related issues.
- ✔ *www.americanheart.org* – This site provides information on the American Heart Association.

Mental Health

- ✔ *www.anad.org* – Information on Anorexia Nervosa and related eating disorders
- ✔ *www.anred.com* – Information on Anorexia Nervosa and related eating disorders

- ✔ *www.healthyminds.org* – American Psychiatric Association (APA) consumer information and locator.

- ✔ *www.overeatersanonymous.org* – Overeaters Anonymous is a 12-step peer support program to help lose weight. You can find the nearest meeting by visiting this site.

- ✔ *www.istss.org* – The International Society for Traumatic Stress Studies provides referrals to trauma specialists.

- ✔ *www.nimh.nih.gov* – This government site provides general mental health information.

Smoking Cessation

- ✔ *www.lungusa.org* – The American Lung Association provides Information on smoking cessation.

Note: Pharmaceutical websites also have lots of health-related information. Check out the sites for Pfizer, Lilly, Takeda (diabetes), Merck, Novartis, Abbott Labs, Astra Zeneca, Bristol Myer-Squibb, GlaxoSmithKline, and Johnson & Johnson. If you are on a prescription medication, find out which company makes it and visit its website to learn what the company has to say about your condition. If you are taking a generic version of a brand name drug, find out more about the company that makes the generic version, but also find out more about the brand name drug and contact that pharmaceutical company as well. The companies that produce the brand name medications have a lot of good free stuff so get on their mailing lists. You may even find out about ways to get free or discounted medication and information on clinical trails.

Your Own Notes

What are some of your own ideas and discoveries?

- ✔
- ✔
- ✔
- ✔
- ✔
- ✔
- ✔
- ✔
- ✔
- ✔
- ✔

Glossary

Aerobic Training – One of three types of conditioning that involves any physical activity that increases the heart rate and burns fat calories. Can also be known as cardio.

Anorexia Nervosa – A disease characterized by the refusal to maintain a minimally healthy body weight for age and height along with an intense fear of gaining weight.

Antioxidant – A chemical compound or substance that inhibits oxidation (a process that produces free radicals that can damage cells) and the buildup of fats and oils (cholesterol). Found in fruits and vegetables rich in Vitamins A, C, and E, and linked to reducing breast cancer and heart disease risk.

Beta Carotene – A nutrient found in fruits and vegetables that acts as an antioxidant.

Blood Pressure – The amount of pressure in the arteries, primarily maintained by the contraction of the left ventricle.

Body Mass Index (BMI) – A formula that compares height and weight to determine body size.

Bone Density Test– A scan that measures the porousness of the bones to determine if they are susceptible to fractures and/or brakes.

Bulimia Nervosa – A disease characterized by binge eating and purging behaviors to prevent weight gain.

Calorie – A unit of energy or heat stored in the body that is burned as fuel for functioning.

Carbohydrate – Any group of chemical compounds found in sugars, starches and cellulose.

Cardiovascular - Pertaining to the heart and the blood vessels involved in blood flow circulation.

Cholesterol – A fatty substance in certain foods that ends up in the bloodstream that the body needs to make cell membranes and hormones.

Diabetes – A metabolic disorder that occurs when the body does not produce enough insulin or cannot use the insulin produced, resulting in excess sugar in the bloodstream.

Dietitian – A person with specialized training in diet as it relates to health. Often requires being registered.

Flexibility Training - One of the three types of conditioning the body needs that focuses on muscle stretches.

Free Radicals – By-products of oxidation that cause damage to cells and lead to heart disease and premature aging.

Glucose – A sugary mixture found in certain foods.

Insulin – A hormone secreted by certain cells that regulates carbohydrate metabolism by controlling glucose (sugar) levels in the bloodstream.

Metabolism – A complex physical and chemical process by which cells break down molecules to release energy and heat.

Nutritionist - A person who has studied nutrition, but may not as well-trained as a dietitian.

Obesity – Extremely overweight with a BMI over 30.

Overweight – A BMI score between 25 to 30

Pilates – A method of body-sculpting exercises that involves a few precise movements requiring control and form.

Protein – Complex compounds that contain amino acids, which are essential for the growth and repair of tissue.

Strength Training – One of three types of conditioning that the body needs that involves weightlifting and resistance to tone muscles.

Triglycerides – A type of fat found in the bloodstream that should be below 200 points.

Yoga – Exercises that promote control over the body and mind as part of the Hindu practice aimed at improving consciousness, spiritual insight, and inner peace.

Yo-Yo Dieting Effect – Losing and gaining the same weight over and over again.

Bibliography

Davis, J. "How to Resolve to Eat Better." WebMD. *http://aolsvc.health.webmd.aol.com/content/Article/11/1671_52695.htm.* January 14, 2002.

Davis, J. "Obesity Means Higher Medical Costs." WebMD. *http://aolsvc.health.webmd.aol.com/content/Article/58/66585.htm.* January 13, 2003.

Davis, J. L. "Sugary Foods Making Us Fat." WebMD. *http://aolsvc.health.webmd.aol.com/content/Article/61/71423.htm.* March 4, 2003.

Davis, M., E. Robbins Eshelman, and M. McKay. *The Relaxation & Stress Reduction Workbook.* Oakland, CA: New Harbinger Publications, 1995.

DeNoon, D. "Keep the Weight Off." WebMD. *http://aolsvc.health.webmd.aol.com/content/article/11/1671_52694.htm.* December 31, 2001.

DeNoon, D. "Stealth Fat Lurks in Favorite Foods." WebMD. February 10, 2003.

Droze, K. "Effective Fitness: The Ten Commandments." eDiets. *http://www.ediets.com/news/article.cfm?code=24567&article_id=7202.* February 1, 2003.

Faelten, S. *Food and You.* Emmaus, PA: Rodale Press, 1996.

Ellis, A., and M. Abrams. *How to Cope with a Fatal Illness.* New York: Barricade Books, 1994.

Grayson, C. E. "Keeping the Weight Off." Cleveland Clinic, *http://aolsvc.health.webmd.aol.com/content/article/2731.1653*. October 28, 2002.

Healthwise. "Healthy Weight." *http://aolsvc.health.webmd.aol.com?content/healthwise/103/25522.htm.* January 4, 2003

Heavin, G., and C. Colman. *Curves: Permanent Results without Permanent Dieting.* New York: Putnam's Sons, 2003.

Kemper, D. W. *Healthwise Handbook.* Boise, ID: Healthwise Publication, 1995.

Kirchheimer, S. "Protein Diet May Prompt Weight Loss: Amino Acid in Animal Protein Burns Fat, Spares Muscle." WebMD. *http://aolsvc.health.webmd.aol.com/content/article/60/67178.htm*. February 25, 2003.

Mayo Clinic Health Oasis. "Obesity in America." *http://www.cnn.com/2000/HEALTH?mayo/10/05/obesity.america*. January 2, 2003.

Net.Content. "Ten Tips of Encouragement." *http://aolsvc.health.webmd.aol.com/content/pages/6/3220_238.htm. Net.Content*. 1999.

Peeters, A., et al. "Obesity in Adulthood and Its Consequences for Life Expectancy: A Life-Table Analysis." *Annals of Internal Medicine* 138 (2003): 24–32.

O'Shea, M. "What Exercise Program Do You Recommend for a Seriously Out of Shape Baby Boomer?" *Parade Magazine* 8 (2003).

Prevention: Women's Health Today. Emmaus, PA: Rodale Press, 2003.

Schlosberg, S. "Sensible New Year's Workouts." WebMD. *http://aolsvc.health.webmd.aol.com/content/Article/14/1676_50193.htm.* January 11, 2000.

Swan, P. B. "Metabolism." World Book Online Americas Edition. *http://www.worldbookonline.com?ar?/na/ar/co/ar357720.htm.* January 5, 2003.

U.S. Department of Health and Human Services Agency for Healthcare Research and Quality. *The Pocket Guide to Good Health for Adults.* Washington, DC: Agency for Healthcare Research and Quality, 2003.

INDEX

N

O

P

Q

R

S

Can You?

Tell us what you can too do! Future volumes of *You Can Too* are under way. We are developing a *You Can Too Inspire Others* book and are looking for stories that will help motivate and teach others to live healthier, so tell us what you do to get and stay healthy. We are also collecting healthy recipes for a *You Can Too Cook* book. You may send photos with your submissions. All published submissions will give credit to the author. Please include a self-addressed stamped envelope with your submission. Please send submissions to:

Resilient Press
11921 Georgia Avenue
PO Box 130
Wheaton, MD 20902
FAX: 301-570-2279
Online: *www.YC2.org*

LECTURES AND SEMINARS

Contact us at the listed addresses to schedule speaking engagements for your company, organization, or group.

About the Author

Jacqueline Garrick has been a health care expert for 20 years. She is a social worker, a Board Certified Expert in Traumatic Stress, and a Certified Personal Trainer. She has helped thousands of people deal with their emotional issues, weight loss and relationships. She has testified before Congress on health related issues and has spoken to audiences internationally. Her own 75-pound weight loss journey inspired her to help others face the problems related to obesity. She is an Army veteran and has her own consulting firm, the FAR Group in the Washington, DC area.

photo by Dennis Tenety

Before

After

photo by Matt Shepley

You Can Too!